Cafés & Coffee Shops

MARTIN PEGLER

No. 2

Cafés & Coffee Shops

MARTIN PEGLER No. 2

VISUAL REFERENCE PUBLICATIONS, INC. · NEW YORK

Visual Reference Publications
302 Fifth Avenue
New York, NY 10001

Distributors to the trade in the United States and Canada
Watson-Guptill Publishers
770 Broadway
New York, NY 10003

Distributors outside the United Sates and Canada
HarperCollins International
10 E. 53rd Street
New York, NY 10022

Library of Congress Cataloging in Publication Data:
Café & Coffee Shops No. 2
Printed in China
ISBN 1-58471-058-6
Designed by Dutton & Sherman

Contents

Introduction

In their Design Business Outlook for the beginning of the 21st century, the editorial board of Contract Magazine agreed that the trends to look for in food service will be more upscale but casually themed dining, the continued popularity of the open kitchen and the entertainment provided by the chefs and their associates, and a warm, cozy and intimate neighborhood feeling in the design. In addition to the above, today's sophisticated diner wants things served up fast, fresh and flavorful—healthy—and maybe even a little exotic. The younger consumers, in their 20s and 30s, are having a marked impact on the restaurant industry and more and more they are the ones who the restaurateurs and café/cafeteria designers must please.

In this volume, Cafés & Coffee Shops No. 2, we have explored the vast area of casual dining and selected what we think are excellent examples, from literally around the world, to show where the design trends are heading. These projects are the creative efforts of some of the leading architects/designers in the field.

Cafés are becoming more informal and many are theme based. We have casual dining with an Asian/Fusion slant, a Seafood/Cuban look, and more cafés are giving "couch potatoes" a reason to get away from the TV at home and get involved and watch sports on TV in some sports memorabilia-filled dining room. Camaraderie and good-neighbor feelings are natural in brewery/pub/café settings.

Food courts used to mean a location in a mall or shopping center, but the concept has expanded far beyond that and also has become more personalized. By combining several suppliers or concessionaires of different but compatible foodstuffs, the diner-on-the-run can pick and choose between an American burger, a Chinese rice dish, a Louisiana po' boy, Japanese sushi, a Mexican taco wrap, or any kind of fried chicken, soups, salads and baked goods. Food courts are also appearing on busy streets in downtown shopping and financial districts as well as in commercial buildings and in giant corporate buildings located in remote industrial parks or along major highways. Visitors to sports arenas can opt for something other than just a hot dog and a soft drink. Colleges and universities are now serving their students in multinational, multi-taste, cafeterias that not only offer freshly prepared foods but also have wit, whimsy and style. These food courts not only provide food selection but offer a variety of seating options, convenience, comfort and great ambiance.

The projects selected serve unique, different and specialized menus in cafés, diners, delicatessens, coffee shops, cafeterias and at fast food stands. The designers had to attract, promote and sell the "brand" name as well as present the wares and still satisfy the requirements of food production and health codes. That took Store Design, Merchandise Presentation, Graphics & Signage, and every trick in the design vocabulary. We believe these designers and architects have succeeded admirably in pleasing their clients and the targeted consumers. We hope you find turning these pages an enlightening, stimulating, thought-provoking and mouth watering experience.

Martin M. Pegler

Cafés & Coffee Shops

MARTIN PEGLER No. 2

Baang

"The name Baang—meaning in Chinese 'to bind or tie together'–signifies the blending of French with Asian cuisine and Asian design interpreted whimsy." The simple exterior of Baang on a walking street in Aspen, CO, features a revolving door and two copper clad barn doors that slide open to reveal the warm glow of the mica columns inside. One gets the feeling of stepping out of the casual, outdoor lifestyle of Aspen and into the sophistication of Manhattan.

David Rockwell and the Rockwell Group of New York City, the designers of Baang, avoided the use of primary colors as they would not evoke the feeling of fusion that the

DESIGN • Rockwell Group, New York, NY
DAVID ROCKWELL • Principal in charge
PHOTOGRAPHY • Paul Warchol , New York, NY

designers hoped to express. Instead they used the authentic colors derived from spices used in Chinese cuisine: ginger root yellow, chili pepper red and the leek green tonality that was used on the walls and floor of Baang. Oxidized, hand-crafted metals were added as accents and highlighters. The exposed kitchen, dining room and bar are all captured in one open, 3200 sq. ft. space that still manages to offer patrons a feeling of intimacy where they can socialize and watch the continuous show in the kitchen and around the bar. The bar is clad in antique vintage linoleum and highlighted by the graceful mica bar lamps. The view into the kitchen is especially good from the grand banquette which is situated directly in front of it. The designers, inspired by Asian pagodas, created the soft "clouds" that flow throughout the space and rest on the glowing amber and gold mica columns. The "clouds" are imprinted with gentle silhouettes of aspen tree leaves.

Upstairs, in the Satay Bar Lounge that is actually an over-hanging mezzanine space, there are cozy loveseats and casual seating which adapt to the use of ski groups. In the V.I.P. dining area, the photography of Steven Richter is featured. They are scenes from the travels in Asia of this Aspen/New York photographer and they are beautifully illuminated from above.

When the weather permits, 12 ft. tall zinc covered hangar doors slide back and guests can enjoy patio seating—like in a café in Paris or New York. The restaurant also features a side arbor lined with potted trees and hanging hurricane lamps.

Riki Tiki Tavi

MANCHESTER, UK

T hings aren't so staid and Victorian in Manchester, England as they once were. Located in one of the Old World enclosed shopping arcades is a new and exciting café that features "street foods" of East Asia. Designed by Akar Studios of Santa Monica, CA, the name—Riki Tiki Tavi—was taken from Rudyard Kipling's "The Jungle Book."

The second floor café is situated in what is now the Printworks Entertainment District and the fun begins with the colorful signage at street level. The bright yellow and white, neon outlined letters stand out from the red, pink and yellow backlit panels. A curry colored wall that leads to the elevator is highlighted with Asian masks which will reappear in a mural upstairs. The "sculpture-like" entrance of curved and angled metal beams frame the modern elevator with an old, industrial style staircase surrounding it.

Inside, the café is bright and energetic—"a playful melange of vibrant colors and textures." Design with economy in mind and with making it a fun place to be, the designers filled the open space with bright, hot colors: curry, paprika and other spicy accent colors. Ultramarine blue is the cooling, contrast color and it appears on the overhead shapes and the upholstered banquettes. The first impression the visitor has is of the high industrial ceiling filled with a "giant kaleidoscope of luminous forms." The large diamond shaped panels are suspended throughout the space at various planes and assorted angles. These camouflage the

pipes, vents and other utilities that run overhead. The backlit forms create "a brilliant structure resembling kites in flight." A 20 ft. mural in cyclamen pink is filled with colorful renditions of Asian masks and the mural along with the three oversized bay windows that overlook the center's internal courtyard and the street are focal points in the design.

Columns are clad in earthy beige ceramic squares and the wood floor picks up the yellowish cast which contrasts with the deep red patterns on the stained floor. Bright red, as well as ultramarine blue, fabrics are used to upholster the banquettes especially those near the windows and red is also used on some feature walls and piers. The bar area is highlighted by the many suspended and unusual light forms that simulate the idea of the Tibetan prayer wheels.

Riki Tiki Tavi opened only a few short months ago and already the café has made a strong imprint on the fun 'n 'food seekers in the new Manchester.

DESIGN • Akar Studio, Santa Monica, CA

SAT GARG, AIA • Design Principal

DESIGN TEAM • Alberico Mele • Project Designer
  Kristi Jack • Designer
  Anna Steiner • Interior Sourcing &Research

PHOTOGRAPHY • Christine Ferni & Julie Fletcher

Naked Fish

BOSTON, MA

The Naked Fish wood-fired grill is located in a long and narrow space in the Bostonian Hotel in Boston. In addition to a bar/lounge and a dining room, the space also was required to feature an open kitchen. The challenge, in addition to the spatial one, was to create the proper setting for this unique concept; an unusual seafood menu to be spiked with Caribbean motifs and to capture the vibrant energy and excitement of the current Latin-Cuban trend. The idea was "to transport diners to a warmer Havana climate."

Without resorting to "stereotypical details and imagery," the designers at JBD of Warwick, RI combined the natural essence of the ocean with the tempo of a night-dinner club. The color palette is filled with assorted blues and yellows set off by off-white, natural woods and stainless steel. Panels of blue translucent plastic float overhead and camouflage the

dropped acoustical tiled ceiling. The off-white ceramic tile floor is set off by squares of smaller yellow tiles while blue ceramic tiles are used to border the partial divider that separates the serpentine bar from the dining area. Sculpted stainless steel waving forms—like sea growths or kelp—create a semi screen. Hanging from the ceiling, in front of the open kitchen, is a blue, wave-like ceiling fixture. Blue glass tiles also appear as a base board around the counter in front of the kitchen as well as the foot rest of the bar. The bar is clad with panels of yellow stained wood and the top of the bar is trimmed with bands of blue mosaic tiles Completing the color scheme are the yellow column, piers and the pull back draperies.

Large 6 x 6 stick posts help to create a unique room with interior dining spaces. The upholstered booth seating plays up the greenish yellow color while the exposed framework is finished in blue. The tinted concrete floor of the dining room is awash with waves and swirling patterns in yellow, blues and greens with occasional accent tiles set into the floor.

The design team did their research in Havana and documented interior colors and art pieces and then incorporated the realistic Cuban details into the design. The details exemplify the fun and energy of the food and music of Havana and combined with ocean iconography they establish Naked Fish as a unique architectural space.

DESIGN • JBD, Warwick, RI
DESIGN TEAM • Glenn Lepore/Peter Boscio/Rebecca Dormady
PHOTOGRAPHY • Warren Jagger Photography, Inc.

Fox Sports Sky Box

SKY HARBOR INT'L. AIRPORT, PHOENIX, AZ

Just as ham goes with eggs, sports and sporting events naturally team up with cafés and "watering holes." Appearing, as though by popular demand, in airports around the U.S., are Fox Sports Sky boxes. Following the popularity of the one that opened in Staples Center in Los Angeles, Fox Sports and HMS Host have, with the design capabilities of AAD of Scottsdale, been opening Sports Sky Boxes in Chicago, New York, Las Vegas and now, this one, in Phoenix.

"Using the familiar Fox Sports imagery and translating it into architectural design elements is what helped create the excitement of Fox Sports Sky Box," says Colette Postlmayr of AAD. "The process of the design is ever-evolving and is designed to mirror the visual elements and icons featured on Fox Sports." Most of the Sky Box operations are located in airports in spaces of approximately 1500 sq ft. The feeling is that of being in a Fox Sports television studio and the central terminal of TV monitors suggests a video control center and the bar becomes the anchor desk that is featured on Fox NFL

Sunday broadcasts. With 22 different satellite feeds showing sporting events, the ambiance "immediately creates a comfort zone for sports fans familiar with Fox Sports."

Through the brushed steel outlined windows travelers get a view of the activity around the sports-oriented bar and grill in the terminal arcade. The cool color scheme—mostly blue and black with stainless steel accents—sets the relaxed scene and further enhances the atmosphere of the TV studio. LED messages and reports on sporting events traverse the fascia beneath the row of TV monitors over the backlit bar wall. The bar itself is perforated stainless steel with black panels emblazoned with the Fox Sports logo. Adding accents of color to the otherwise monochromatic setting are the "jerseys" and other sports, memorabilia on display in glass cases around the walls.

In keeping with the theme is the "athletic" menu which features "Howie's no-wimp wings," "Terry's Chili-fries," "Collingsworth's grilled chicken salad," as well as hamburgers and sandwiches that reflect the personalities of Fox Sports anchors and stars. "Every aspect of Fox Sports Sky Box is created to showcase Sports Television" and give sports fans-on-the-go a place to stop, to meet, to sip and catch up with what really matters.

DESIGN • AAD, Scottsdale, AZ

EXECUTIVE VP • Michael E. Stevenson, AIA

EXECUTIVE VP • Carl F. Schaffer, AIA

STUDIO DIRECTOR • Nicholas Sherman

DESIGN DIRECTOR • Colette Postlmayer

DEVELOPMENT TEAM • Keith Heinemann/
Keith Ann Laber/Steve Rains/Brett Martin

CLIENT'S DESIGN TEAM

EXECUTIVE VP • Larry Jones

LEVY RESTAURANTS

SR. VP OF DEVELOPMENT • Jeff Wineman

HMS HOST

    VP CONCEPT DEVELOPMENT • Stan Novack

    PHOTOGRAPHY • Norton Photography, Phoenix, AZ

Time Out/American Sports Café

T
ime Out, a popular café/grill/entertainment venue is located in Rome, Italy and it is also known as the American Sports Café. Designed by Studio Cicciotti, the pub/café was inspired by American sports and sports activities "especially the ones that evoke champions and feats familiar to many generations."

Using familiar symbols, icons, props and furnishings associated with American sports, as perceived by the young, trendy and pro-Americans that frequent Time Out, the space has the fun feeling of a theatrical stage set. The designers have relied on cliches and then assembled them in a light-hearted and fanciful manner. There are brick covered walls and walls slatted over with wood. The mostly wood floors are marked off as playing courts or arenas. Cyclone fencing, stainless steel and chromed accents as well as giant, shiny metal vents that

crawl across the open ceiling add to the overall "arena-playground" feeling of the space. According to the designers, the ground division lines on the floor, the trainer's bench and the sports oriented pictures all around are "typically American" and thus make the space "sprightly and unusual."

The American Sports Café features a retro style bar/service counter and a dining area that is a free interpretation of a 1950s-1960s diner. There are several options available at the semi-circular counter set in the center of the space. Guests can order a beer on draught or select something at the coffee/ espresso station. There is also a display of fast foods and snacks. 50's style chrome and naughahyde padded stools are lined up along the bar/counter and booths, also naughahyde upholstered, surround the dining area. The tables are also diner style: Formica tops bound in ribbed steel. The Café is contained behind a partial brick wall topped with cyclone fencing. Stadium style lighting fixtures add to the overall atmosphere as do the graphics of sports figures painted on the brick wall.

Surrounding the fenced-in "America's Cup" (the diner) there are all sorts of activities for the patrons including billiards, pin ball machines, knock-hockey, and computerized and electronic games. To keep things up-to-date, TV monitors are located everywhere and anywhere in Time Out so if a patron doesn't want to play he can watch someone else play. Time Out/American Sports Café brings the 1950s up into the millennium.

DESIGN • Studio Cicciotti, Rome, Italy
PHOTOGRAPHY • Courtesy Studio Cicciotti

Pizzuti Club Lounge

Sportservice, a provider of food service at sports and entertainment facilities, together with the designers at Chute Gerdeman of Columbus developed a range of "fun, fan-friendly food and beverage venues" in the new Nationwide Arena which is the home to the Columbus Bluejackets of the NHL. The Pizzuti Lounge & Club Bar is on the Club level and the Bud Light Terrace Food Court, shown further on in this edition, is on the main concourse.

The 9650 sq. ft. Pizzuti Lounge is a "more exclusive" experience at the attack twice end of the arena while the Club Bar is on the side near the loge boxes. To keep this upscaled café area consistent with the "timeless architectural character" of

the arena, the designers mixed traditional wood with high-tech stainless steel. Highlighting the area is the sensational curved bar unit clad in variegated copper. A backlit form of white translucent glass swells up from the back bar and reaches up to the ceiling—passing the mezzanine level. This illuminated "funnel, outlined and delineated in stainless steel, serves as a beacon for the lounge. Radiating out from this illuminated element are concentric bands of stainless steel that create a dynamic canopy over the bar area.

In the casual seating areas, between the various service counters, a metal grid drops down to create a sense of intimacy which is reinforced by the dimmed down lighting. The polished concrete floors are marked off by sweeping arcs of a rich blue color and that same signature blue appears in the neon and in the textured glass fillers of the ceiling grids. The soft blue light envelops the area and adds to the exclusiveness of the space. Illuminated niches, cut into the white walls, are filled with decorative yellow and blue glass bottles as well as jars of imported condiments, oils and vinegars. The yellow and blue bottles also are decoratively displayed in the illuminated cases in the copper clad counters.

DESIGN • Chute Gerdeman, Columbus, OH
PHOTOGRAPHY • Michael Houghton, StudiOhio, Columbus, OH

Speedway Café

changes and there is a glow emanating from the many video monitors that frame the "open" glass storefront and the "mechanistic" inspired dining room is on full view.

The ceiling from the exterior dining patio extends inside and bends downward to contain a bank of video monitors and booth seating beneath. The color scheme echoes the racing/track colors of bright chrome yellow and black with accents of a variety of shades of gray and silvery metal highlights. In addition to the yellow laminate covered booths with the gray/black upholstery and chrome used for an accent, there are also the highly polished, black laminate topped tables with "ant" chairs in black and chrome designed by Arne Jacobsen.

A curvilinear "graphic" wall slopes downward to reveal the open kitchen and the soffit above is filled with more TV monitors and memorabilia. Also overhead—and surrounding the dining area—are actual racing cars that "reinforce the linear motion of the restaurant." The curved bar is highlighted by its bright orange glossy front and the stainless steel top. A strip of shiny orange vinyl inlay in the floor surrounds the bar and defines the cocktail lounge as "a dynamic space for interac-

Irvine Spectrum is one of the largest and most exciting entertainment/retail centers in the U.S. and located amidst the Spanish and Moorish influenced architectural designs is Speedway Café designed by Space International. This restaurant is the largest of the international chain of theme restaurants based on high speed motor sports and the challenge to the designers was to fit the high technology usually associated with racing into this complex. The designers created a buffer zone with a linear outdoor dining area facing the center's courtyard and this separates the café's contrasting materials from those of the themed surroundings. From the patio, Indie racing cars serve as a shading device for the outdoor diners as the cars are elevated on hydraulic lifts. At night the "story"

tion." Stools made of yellow coils of metal surrounding a vertical support are accentuated by the black and yellow seat covers.

Seen overhead is the blacked-out ceiling and the exposed silvery HVAC ducts and pipes that "mimic the exhaust pipe for a top fuel dragster." An actual one appears on the wall over the bar and the wall of TV monitors, backlit photos and memorabilia. The dragster was donated by Budweiser and "Bud" banners as well as other beer logos hang throughout the booth seating area. Simple white cylindrical light cannisters hang down over the seating along with sharp, exposed bulbs that appear like "stars" in the black firmament above.

DESIGN • Space International, Los Angeles, CA
PHOTOGRAPHY • Michael Ferguson

Compari's-on-the-Park

PLYMOUTH, MI

The 3600 sq. ft. space, located in a strip center, was designed by Marco Design Group of Northville MI to be an "upscale Italian restaurant that offers professionals a stylish atmosphere for lunch while morphing into a cozy family café in the evening." To accomplish this, the designers used a sophisticated mix of colors, patterns and materials within the confines of the existing building. The result is "a rich, yet dazzling environment" that is also warm, intimate and inviting."

Adding to the cozy quality are the curvilinear booths upholstered in multicolored fabric. Bold colors such as saffron gold and midnight blue are used to delineate the dining space which is further enhanced by the worm wood accents that also appear in other areas of the restaurant/café. Custom made metal accents decorate the multi-partitioned booths and the

curved bar which is oak stained dark cherry and enriched with blue glass mosaic tiles. The bar is also enhanced by the complementary arced ceiling above it and the curved metal wine racks and light sconces. In this area, imported Italian porcelain tiles are laid on the floor. Separating the tiled bar area from the carpeted seating area are partitions of tambour wood stained cherry and capped with wrought metal swirls. An old brick wall, on one side, adds to the informal, intimate and cozy feeling for the booths lined up next to it.

A light-hearted feeling is added with the detailing. There is a whimsical mural of a fantasy Venetian scene painted on the exterior wall over the main entrance. It conveys "a fun, food message" and adds character to the restaurant's exterior that stretches across two existing storefronts. Inside there are hand painted murals of authentic Italian "food" cliches on the walls as well as a photo of the café's founding fathers on the back wall near the kitchen. "It gives the diner a sense of familiarity while in the space." Hanging over the hostess station is a "pasta strainer" lamp and Murano glass lighting fixtures in a variety of colors and sizes are strategically placed around the room to create different moods; from cozy and intimate to informal and casual.

Since Compari's is located in the center of an historical downtown area on a heavily trafficked street, a fenced-in outdoor café was created so that diners can enjoy the view of the park across the way while dining al fresco.

DESIGN • Marco Design Group, Northville, MI
  Nicholas Giammarco/Julie Dugas/Nada Abbate
VISUAL MERCHANDISING • Viz Biz, Royal Oak, MI
MURALS • Mind's Eye Studio, Sterling Heights, MI
PHOTOGRAPHY • Laszlo Regos Photography, Berkley, MI

New Age Café

The inspiration for the New Age Café in Rome was the name itself. The designers, Studio Cicciotti, wanted to create a place that reflects the life and the activity of today in a traditional Italian bar/café in a city that has withstood the ravages of time. Located in the central zone of this metropolis, during the daylight hours it is frequented by people who work in the area. They will drop in for a coffee or espresso, a quick lunch or a quicker drink of something stronger. However, at night the complexion changes as does the clientele. When the sun goes down the young and the fun-loving come out and find the fun places to go. New Age Café is one of them.

According to the designers, there is no special theme—"almost like a New Age philosophy" but it "is organized aesthetically and architectonically structured in such a way that the customer himself may decide how to live in it, by eating at

DESIGN: Studio Ciccotti, Rome, Italy
PHOTOGRAPHY: Courtesy of Studio Ciccotti

the counter—at the high tables—or sitting quietly on the gallery floor." The building itself has a sweeping, curved end so the café is actually semi-circular in plan as well. Through the large glazed entrances one can see the two level interior and the focal bar at the back end under the overhanging gallery seating. Heartwood and ceramics are used to affect the look of the worn wood, pieced floors and the brick faced walls, wrought metal balustrades and multi-colored, broken tile mosaics add to the overall look of the space.

The bar top curves and undulates in and out and it combines a service/counter with a display of prepared foods and snacks at the far end. Tall stools with slate blue upholstered seats are pulled up to the bar and the footrest is a wave-like platform finished with a mosaic of colored tiles—blue predominating. TV monitors, located over the bar, afford the diner the opportunity of watching videos, listening to music or just socializsing.

To play up the gallery seating, the designers opened up the iron, load-bearing trusses to view, and made them an integral part of the design. They bring the patron's eye up to the fanciful wrought iron balustrade and the secluded seating behind. "The design concept of this project generally reflects our philosophy for creating cutting-edge and original public houses/cafés where the customer may derive pleasure and be attracted and tempted by the surroundings."

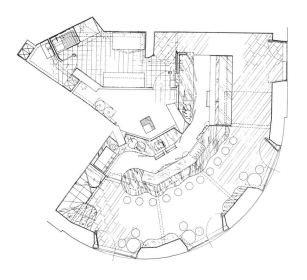

Gordon Biersch Brewery/Café

LAGUNA HILLS, CA

The popular Gordon Biersch Brewery/Café in laguna Hills, CA is located in what was once a bank building in the days before ATM machines. It is at the edge of a suburban mall parking lot. The architects/designers of this project, Allied Architecture & Design of San Francisco, peeled away the existing interior walls, ceilings and finishes to reveal "a building with a barn-like clarity; four masonry blocks walls spanned by heavy timber trusses, supporting a high, gabled roof."

The brewery/café was structured around an "existing cruciform diagram set by large concrete arched openings" at the centers of each of the four block walls. The designers added a central free-standing volume of brick to define two of the three major "programmatic" elements of Bar and Dining, and yet maintained the "one large room nature" of the existing shell. The third "program" is the working brewery which now weaves in and out of the north wall. It not only "activates" the bar and dining areas but the inner workings are revealed to the street through the large glazed areas.

Many of the interior design cues (for colors and materials) are based on German beer brewing traditions. "handcrafting" and "authenticity" matter! Rich mahogany wood is used for the millwork throughout and it is traditionally detailed as on the deep paneled and profiled bar, on the wainscoting, and the built-in seating. Hand wrought iron railings and brackets provide "an organic sensibility" and they are highlighted by the abstract imagery of wheat and barley. To create areas of intimacy inside the open spatial volume, wood trellises appear at the bar and in the dining area. They create "a material dialogue between the existing heavy timber elements and the building's new occupation."

The rich golden ocher color of the brew seems to envelop the space and it is complemented by the original brick areas and the rich mahogany woodwork.

DESIGN: Allied Architecture & Design, San Francisco, CA
Martin Austria, Jr./Michael Chen/Roddy Creedon/John B. Lin/Erin Lilly/Kotting Luo/Lih-Chuin Loh/Jeshua Paone/Mark S Schwettman/Bryon Young
PHOTOGRAPHY: Courtesy of Allied Architecture & Design

T.J. Schmid

Targeted at the young urban professionals, T.J. Schmid is an upscale brewery/café with a decidedly urban environment. Located just across from the Arrowhead Pond Events Center and within strolling distance of Edison Field Ball Park, the nature of the "invigorated group of patrons" dictated the brew pub/restaurant's character and decor. As designed by G.S. Beckham Design of Costa Mesa, CA, the undulating granite bar is backed up by 16 ft. high insulated dual pane glass windows detailed with copper mullions. Beyond are the stainless steel brew tanks that provide the "view" as well as the "entertainment."

"The space gives the feeling of sitting in the actual refrigerated serving room of a large brewery." Another focal/entertainment center is the grill line and the open kitchen. At this

"point of energy and excitement," the chefs and staff work beneath three custom copper and milled steel clad exhaust hoods. Overall, there is the atmosphere of a "gentlemen's bar" and that imagery is enhanced by the two tones of wood used throughout the space. The overscaled and bold wood statements are mostly stained a rich, mahogany color. The glass that appears as partitions between the booth seating is chipped and frosted for effect and a bold geometric patterned fabric is used for the upholstery. The fabric boasts of rich earth colors accented with blue and metallic threads. Slate tiles in gray, brown sienna and terra cotta are laid on the floor. Much of the overhead lighting is accomplished by the use of cable lighting which leaves the ceiling open and "unfinished"—as in a warehouse or brewery. The "industrial" quality of the design is contrasted with the elegance of the natural and traditional woodwork.

A patio with a bar-b-que grill and a bar of its own is set amidst a "jungle of tropical foliage" and "the pre-game events create an enthusiasm and electricity that carries over into the restaurant."

DESIGN • G.S. Beckham Designs, Costa Mesa, CA
PHOTOGRAPHY • Scott Rothwell, Costa Mesa, CA

Library Alehouse

The Library Alehouse is situated on a main street in downtown Santa Monica in an area called the Ocean Park district. The renovated café makes its presence known on the street of mostly rehabbed Art Deco and Art Moderne buildings by its unique shopfront which features a tilted, trellis-like grid sun screen that stretches across most of the cream stucco facade. The translucent "awning" is reminiscent of the Japanese, shallow pitched roof lines of some of the homes in this area. "The detailed joinery of the store front announces the skewed geometry of the 'ridge beam' which moves the patron from Main St. to the interior dining room and bar."

The light wood and the color accents of the facade "embrace the space" as they continue the palette of materials inside. The clear, fresh and open interior combines the warm, glowing wood tones of a variety of exotic hardwoods with cool metallic surfaces to achieve a sophisticated balance and form an "abstracted craftsman environment." The timber construction elements that fly across the ceiling recall the exterior grid/awning. One side wall is sheathed in wood and Mission-style lanterns hang off it. On a high shelf that runs the length of the long wall, is a display of antique and not-so-antique beer and ale bottles. The fine woodworking techniques that distinguished the Craftsman period and the Mission style of the early 20th century is also evident in the treatment of the bar that fills the left side of the space. A large portion of the quilted metal clad wall—at the end of the bar—contains a line of taps for the assorted beers and ales served in the Library Alehouse.

Set in the brick wall, at the end of the room, is a door that leads to an out-of-doors patio with a view of the garden. The same lanterns are now suspended from the sloping, tent-like ceiling and the floor is covered with cement tiles.

DESIGN • Space International, Los Angeles, CA
PHOTOGRAPHY • Benny Chan

Café Winberie

Aumiller-Youngquist, the noted restaurant designers based in Mt. Prospect, IL, were challenged by the client, the Ownership Group, to revitalize an existing 6500 sq. ft. space which was previously 60% bar and 40% restaurant. In addition to bringing the restaurant area into prominence, the client wanted Café Winberie to have the ambiance of a French brasserie—with Mediterranean design influences.

As redesigned, the small bar which can seat ten to 12 patrons, is at the rear of the dining room and the seating area directly around it can either serve as bar seating or, if needed, be part of the dining room seating. "The bar acts as the initial and main point when entering the restaurant." Flanking the main dining area are smaller dining zones and a private dining room. Two additional smaller private dining rooms, which can accommodate six to eight guests, are located up front near the entry. Operable red velvet drapery accord them privacy and these rooms are often requested for small, special occasions.

Cream colored walls and off-white travertine floors with granite medallion accents open up the space. Highlighting and enriching the café is the mahogany trim, wainscot, accents and the wood lined ceiling. Custom designed light fixtures in the ceiling define the dining space. Wood bistro chairs and booth seating are provided in the restaurant area while in the bar there are granite topped tables with leather and rattan dining chairs.

Adding to the brasserie feeling are the brass accents; the railings on the half walls between the booths and the light fixtures with French Nouveau details. French lace window treatments and the European poster art and reproductions of French masters are other "bistro/brasserie" decorative elements added to the design. Nouveau millwork details are used throughout; on the hostess station, the railings, wine cases, the service stations and the back bar.

DESIGN • Aumiller-Youngquist, Mt. Prospect, IL
PRINCIPAL IN CHARGE • David Kasprak
DESIGN TEAM
  PROJECT MANAGER • Leigh Maraviglia
  INTERIOR DESIGN • Lindsay Davis
  PHOTOGRAPHY • Ed Massery, Massery Photography, Inc.

The Pickle Barrel

To turn an awkward 15,000 sq.ft. health club into a relaxing and amusing, family-friendly restaurant/café took a lot of creative design magic. The magician was the Hirschberg Design Group of Toronto. With a seating capacity of 320 persons, it meant a lot of movement in and out and around the space. Because of that and the unusual space configuration, the designers created a major aisle with secondary aisles leading to the various seating zones. In addition to being a full service facility, there is a large retail deli/take-out area for quality meals-to-go or for the purchasing of the Pickle Barrel's famous sauces and dressings. In laying out the assorted parts of Pickle Barrel—the restaurant/café, the deli/take-out and the seating, the designers accommodated the "awkward" floor plan.

Throughout the space one is aware of the rich textures of oxidized and patterned copper. The copper is combined with flowing patterns of vivid stained glass and a beautiful, backlit liquor wall to create a striking background for the 50 ft. long bar. Whimsical art and glass mosaic tile set in unusual designs add to the fantasy setting. These are underscored by the detailed rosebud iron-work that further reinforces the light-hearted feeling. The odd shaped columns are covered with yellow and black tiles and they look like stylized tulips. The same colors appear on the bar front which is complemented by the yellow wood bar stools.

Semi-circular booths provide a sense of privacy out in the middle of the floor. Orange and maroon stained woods cover the outer circumference of the booths while the seats are upholstered in a happy print. The same wood colors are used on the front of the service counter that frames the open kitchen. The assorted food stations are treated with different appliques of glass tiles; triangles of orange and blue cover the soup and juice counter while there are multi-colored squares used to decorate the take-out and dessert stations. To top it all off, the blacked-out ceiling is camouflaged by floating disks of assorted colors.

DESIGN • Hirschberg Design Group, Toronto, ON
PHOTOGRAPHY • Interior Images

Rosa Mexicana

Success breeds success and for Doug Griebel and Dan Hickey it meant opening a newer, bigger and even more colorful Rosa Mexicana restaurant/café on the upper west side of Manhattan to complement their established east side venue. Commissioned to execute the 6,000 sq. ft., dual level restaurant design was David Rockwell of The Rockwell Group.

The new location, opposite Lincoln Center on W. 62nd St.—in the cultural hub of New York City—features a blend of Mexican cuisine and Mexican arts in a colorful, contemporary setting devised by Rockwell. Upon entering, the diner is greeted by a 30 ft. tall, two-level "water wall" of shimmering iridescent glass mosaic tiles that ombre from a rich, deep blue color to a soft lavender hue. As a whimsical note—and a subtle reference to the cliff divers of Acapulco—200 miniature divers are lined up and about to dive-a la a Busby Berkley production number off the wall that is as focal point on both lev-

---

DESIGN • The Rockwell Group
DESIGNER • David Rockwell, principal
LIGHTING DESIGN • Paul Gregory, Focus Lighting, Inc.
PHOTOGRAPHY • Paul Warchol, New York, NY

els. According to the research conducted by David Rockwell and David Mexico, of the design firm, "We found that in every hacienda or town square there was a fountain. This provided a natural feature that we strongly felt should anchor our design. In this case the water wall and the divers provided the guests with different images from up close and from a distance." Paul Gregory of Focus Lighting planned the lighting for the restaurant and, by the use of special lamps and filters, achieved an effect of a "sculptural wall" that "sparkles with light glinting off the thin sheet of moving water and the reflections of the divers."

Tiles of assorted hot colors and sizes and in various patterns are used throughout the restaurant/café and they are complemented by the soft, sheer flowing draperies that are illuminated to created glowing areas along the perimeter of the space. The bar area, set near the entrance, is distinguished by the border of hot pink tiles set in front of the bar which is clad with multicolored mosaic glass tiles. The back of the bar has back lit panels of rose petals suspended in resin and walls and shelves finished in cyclamen pink lacquer. They add to

the flush and glow of the space that is illuminated by custom, wire mesh encased glass cylinder lamps.

Another spectacular focal point in the design is the floating stairway that connects the two levels. It consists of slabs of orange terrazzo alternating with red slabs and it steps off from a pad of the same deep blue tiles that appear on the adjacent water wall previously mentioned. Aisles and walkways are delineated by a checkerboard pattern of orange and cream colored tiles.

Rosa Mexicana sends out a warm, welcoming glow of gold, orange, pink and red that is balanced by the cool blues. The walls, ceilings and flooring emanate a feeling of sunshine and the arts and crafts of Mexico beautifully presented in niches and against colored panels—all precisely and dramatically lit—add to the dining experience. The blend of the art and the architecture and the total setting by the Rockwell group creates a "visceral, tactile relationship between the guest and the environment." "Our lives are so full of sensory overload," says Rockwell, "that our desire was to entertain people with an obsessively beautiful atmosphere."

Park Classic Diner

There once was a "sort of, kind of," diner-type restaurant located on this corner in Jeanette, PA. It was a highly visible and trafficked location, but the existing structure just wasn't doing it. The client wanted to see a 1950s diner on that spot and that is what he got when JBD of Warwick, RI took over the renovation assignment.

The Park Classic Diner is actually a prototype design for the Eat'N'Park diners. The new "old" design is filled to overflowing with the wonderful, nostalgic signature elements of diner design from half a century ago. It all starts with the brilliant facade design with its glitz and glitter of the diamond patterned metal surfacing, the vaulted roof and the blaze of red and blue neon that only shimmer in daylight but come up in full glory at night. Inside it is "Back to the Future" or Retro-Revisited. The main area is covered by a

gently-arced ceiling and the floor is patterned with a red and yellow checkerboard design set into a warm beige inlaid floor. Bright blue tiles edge the floor along the row of upholstered booths that feature upholstery in red, yellow and blue. True to the diner tradition, the Formica topped tables are supported on chromed legs and are banded with a shiny corrugated metal trim. Separating the booths are crinkle glass partitions in metal frames. The long counter/service/bar is inlaid with white tiles accented with red and yellow and bordered in blue. The patterned silvery panels on the fascia over the opening to the kitchen carries the "traditional" neon outlined clock. Blue and yellow conical glass lamps hang over the counter and neon lighting reinforces the retro diner look. A really fun touch—and a very popular feature—is the mural along one long wall by Toucan Graphics and the mottoes and words of wisdom that appear as a trim just under the ceiling.

DESIGN • JBD Judd Brown Designs, Warwick, RI

PROJECT MANAGER • Mark Palazio

DIRECTOR OF DESIGN • Glenn Lepore

INTERIOR DESIGN • Leah Wheary

PHOTOGRAPHY • Warren Jagger Photography, Inc.

Katzenberg Express

The Katzenberg Express is the more styled and colorful relative of Katzenberg's which is the more formal restaurant/ delicatessen located on a main street in Greenwich, CT. As designed by Haverson Architecture & Design of Greenwich, the new deli/café "enjoys a warm, comfortable atmosphere complemented by stylized design elements reminiscent of the early '60's."

The Katzenberg family has for generations satisfied the deli cravings of this upscale community and six generations of the family now look down from the walls in photographs brightly matted in lime, teal, lemon yellow and cherry red. The frames were selected to complement the portraits and the period when they were taken thus "creating a collage designed to reinforce the homey, light-hearted ambiance." Included in the store's design are a vivid color scheme, built-in, curved counters with futuristic styled stools for seating, and suspended cabinets along the walls. Diners may sit at a service counter up front or on a banquette covered in a bold coral colored fabric that repeats the boomerang pattern of the aluminum edged Formica topped tables. There are also tables-for-two to accommodate the lunch and pre-cinema customers.

Sea blue and emerald green mosaic tiles, contained within aluminum frames, define the wall planes, and vintage textured wallcoverings are used on the walls Some walls have built-in niches for the display of period art objects. Lighting plays an important part in the design scheme and the lighting plan includes up-lit kidney shaped ceiling planes, internally lit counter fascias, corkscrew pendants, bullet-head accents and recessed lamps. They all "support and augment a visually rich version of this classic 1960's suburban den of fast delicatessen food."

Retail items such as home-made baked goods, frankfurters, chips, salads and "design-your-own-sandwiches are integrated into the service counter on cylindrical displayers, shelves cantilevered from a floor-to-ceiling pipe and in a cleverly disguised frankfurter cart. The 2000 sq. ft. store was designed as a prototype for a roll-out concept and can seat 50 patrons. Using "sherbet, pop, pre-late 1960's and post diner" colors, maple wood, stainless steel, mosaic tiles, linoleum and plastic laminates the results—as Marc Katzenberg, the owner, states—"When my store was finished I thought I had walked into my Aunt Sylvia's den. I love her house and I love my restaurant."

DESIGN • Haverson Architecture & Design, Greenwich, CT
 Jay Haverson & Carolyn Haverson
PHOTOGRAPHY • Paul Warchol , New York, NY

Dean & De Luca

CHARLOTTE, NC

Aumiller Youngquist was charged by Dean & DeLuca to redefine the original gourmet food concept and create a n design which would work for a nationwide roll-out. The look still had to maintain the basic tenets of the original 1976 store which was located on street level in a loft building on Prince St. in Soho in New York. The look was "industrial" in a brick and concrete setting.

Most important to the design was that the product be the main focus, for and in the space. The space, shown here, is approximately 10,500 sq. ft. in a new, one story retail center in Charlotte, NC. The design is "clean and contemporary" with industrial style fixtures and high tech materials used in the unadorned, off-white volume. The floors are sealed concrete and, for materials, stainless steel is combined with natural wood for the tables, chairs, countertops and as accents.

The open, exposed ceiling is painted-out but dropped ceilings appear over prep areas and service counters to define them, provide a sense of intimacy and human scale while also satisfying the health code issues. "The interior thrusts the kitchen right out to the customer and in no uncertain terms exudes a pride in the quality of the product they are preparing and presenting." Touches such as the revealed wine crates, bushels and baskets and chalkboard menus not only "soften the space" but provide a more personal feeling.

For those who want to taste the exquisitely prepared food or the pre-packaged-to-go, there is a café area where guests can enjoy freshly brewed coffee and a selection of baked goods, made-to-order sandwiches and desserts. A stainless steel service counter/bar, also indentified by a dropped ceiling over it, provides the refreshments. The casual arrangement of wood chairs and tables fill one corner of the space along side the large glazed openings.

DESIGN • Aumiller Youngquist, Mt. Prospect, IL
PRINCIPAL IN CHARGE • Bill Aumiller
PROJECT MANAGER • Leigh Maraviglia
PHOTOGRAPHY • Mark Ballogg, Steinkamp Ballogg Photography

ESPRESSO OFFERINGS
DEAN & DELUCA BRAND

	PICCOLO	ALTO
ESPRESSO	$1.20	$1.40
ESPRESSO MACCHIATTO	$1.20	$1.55
ESPRESSO CON PANNA	$1.25	$1.40
ESPRESSO RISTRETTO	$1.20	

	PICCOLO	ALTO
CAPPUCCINO	$2.15	$2.80
CAFFE LATTE	$2.40	$3.05
CAFFE MOCHA	$2.15	$2.80
LATTE MACCHIATTO	$1.70	$1.90
STEAMER	$0.95	
CAFFE BAMBINO		

BREWED COFFEE
DEAN & DELUCA BRAND

	PICCOLO	ALTO
REGULAR OR DECAF.	$1.15	$1.35
CAFE AU LAIT	$1.25	$1.50
HOT CHOCOLATE	$1.15	$1.35
HOT TEA	$1.25	$1.50

CHILLED BEVERAGES
ICED TEA — $1.50
ICED CAPPUCCINO — $2.50
ORANGE JUICE — $1.65

BEERS AND WINE BY THE GLASS — PRICED INDIVIDUALLY

FLAVORED SYRUPS BY MONIN
CHOCOLATE, VANILLA, CARAMEL, IRISH CREAM,
HAZELNUT, COCONUT, STRAWBERRY, MENTHE, RASPBERRY

Au Bon Pain

Though Au Bon Pain has over 300 outlets spread across the U.S. and as far away as Chile, Brazil, Thailand and Singapore, it was only very recently that the company decided to franchise its name and concept in Canada. They called upon ll X lV Design Associates to take on full design and programming responsibilities for this newer and more sophisticated version of Au Bon Pain.

The menu includes distinctive breads and pastries, which are baked on the premises, as well as specialty soups, salads and sandwiches, and the new concept is attracting not only the usual morning commuters but many lunch and late afternoon diners as well.

This prototype store is located in a 2800 sq. ft. ground level space in an office building in Toronto's financial district. In order to allow daylight and the customer on the street to get "in," the large window is discreetly signed with a sandblasted logo. The view is not of your usual coffee shop! The designers have specified bianca carrera marble, porcelain ceramic tiles, cultured stone, chenille upholstery, flat cut cherry wood veneer and other fine details. The new, lighter and warmer color scheme is evident at once. There is a more spacious feeling due to the toast and honey colored fabrics, the creamy colored floor and the wall finishes that suggest the colors of freshly baked goods. The ll X lV team created more queuing space at the long service and cash counter but also developed a more intimate and cozy ambiance in the seating area where small clusters of white marble topped tables—reminiscent of European patisseries—are arranged. In the lounge zone, patrons can indulge themselves over coffee while relaxing on the fabric covered lounge chairs and read the provided newspapers.

Making a strong and truly sophisticated statement in the café are the dramatic culture stone walls and the mural of the briefcase-toting executives. Lighting, as always, plays an important part in creating the desired feeling and here the lights are positioned for the behind-the-counter tasks, to highlight the product presentation and enhance the relaxed ambiance of the dining area. Custom "lampshades," in two different kinds of groupings and sizes, act as decorative accents as well as effective light diffusers.

DESIGN • ll X lV Design Associates, Toronto, ON
PHOTOGRAPHY • David Whittaker

Choices

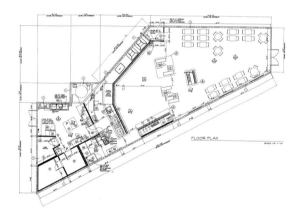

FLOOR PLAN

ARCHITECT/DESIGNER • The Tricarico Group, Wayne, NJ

OWNER • Nicholas J. Tricarico

PROJECT ARCHITECT/DESIGNER • John Pandolfino

FINISH SELECTION • Laura Calvetto

PROJECT MANAGER • Joe Avallone

FOR AU BON PAIN

   PROJECT MANAGER • Yong Moon Han

   PHOTOGRAPHY • Andrea Brizzi

Choices Restaurant is a subsidiary of Au Bon Pain and when The Tricarico Group was asked to create the prototype design, their objective was to develop an environment that would be "as refreshing as your morning's first cup of coffee." This self-serve café offers patrons a selection of freshly baked items, sandwiches and salads.

The foods are beautifully displayed in display cases on the user-friendly self-service counters. To draw the diner to the plentiful arrangement of foodstuffs, there are oversized matching and complementary graphics on both side walls that lead the diner to the rear of the space where the counters are located. The back wall—behind the service area—and the walls in the full service kitchen are covered with 4 x 4 rustic glazed tiles in an assortment of terra cotta, earth tones—"to create an inviting backdrop" for the food display.

The round and square tables have wood grained laminate tops and they sit on the light, off-white tiled floor which is accented with areas of terra cotta tiles. The creamy walls and ceiling add to the wide open, clean feeling of the rather large store. Ocher gold colored ceiling beams cut across the seating area and visually cuts that area into smaller, more intimate zones. The reddish brown wood chairs, upholstered in black, go with the black bases and nosing around the light wood table tops. The giant paintings spaced along both side walls add touches of color but mostly accentuate the ocher of the ceiling beams.

In addition to the recessed fluorescent fixtures in the ceiling, unusual, squarish-shaped pendant lamps are suspended throughout to create a warm ambient light while track lights, along the perimeter walls, highlight the murals. "This specialty food, self service café offers the patrons a lively yet sophisticated atmosphere with the use of bright reflective colors and finishes."

Ralph's La Jolla Village Café

RALPH'S MARKETPLACE, LA JOLLA CA.

In keeping with the trends and the shoppers' desires for something different, Ralph's Marketplace—a destination for discriminating shoppers of fine gourmet and specialty foods—has included a Village Café where the shopper can withdraw for some quiet time—some refreshment time and even catch up on his/her reading time—or just surf the internet. It is all here as here in the La Jolla Village Café as designed by Brown, Bunyan, Moon and More.

DESIGN • Brown, Bunyan, Moon and More, Glendale, CA
    Jeri Montalvo • Principal & Director of Design
DESIGN TEAM • Mei Chin/Mark Tasse/Diane Haber
PHOTOGRAPHY • Smith Photography, Santa Ana, CA

This café-within-the-store incorporates a full service gourmet coffee bar, café seating, some cozy and intimate reading nooks as well as six computer stations for on-line browsing. The attached bookstore not only provides reading material for the coffee-sippers but books and magazines to be purchased and taken away. Using "traditional home elements and modern technology" such as hand stained woodwork and crown moldings, glazed ceramic tiles in a rich ocher color behind the service bar, earthy terra cotta tiles on the floor and a mural along one wall of a La Jolla seascape, the designers have created a warm and friendly place to sit, to sip and meet friends.

The Village Café is located within walking distance of the University of California's San Diego campus and thus the café was designed not only to appeal to the college people who shop at Ralph's and have made this area with the available computers an "in" meeting place, but for the retirees and seniors who share the same needs and creature comforts as the younger folk. The warm color palette, the rich finishes and the friendly and enveloping textures all contribute to the Café's popularity as does the indirect and specialty lighting that highlights but also directs shoppers to the product display.

Bellisimo Café

Inspired by an Italian Street café and serving up a simple menu of Italianate dessert specialties and coffee drinks is Bellisimo Café. The café is located in a street level space in North York, ON. The small space, 750 sq. ft., is alive with color and it has a swirling, free and easy feeling about it. The color palette is set with the concrete floor which is a "painted mural" in shades of yellow and gold touched with lavender and green and a design of assorted fruits. Creating a not-to-be-missed path is the uncoiling spiral of multi-colored broken ceramic tiles embedded in the painted and polyurethaned floor. The same tiles, in unbroken condition, create a helter-skelter pattern on the white tile wainscoted long walls. Above, the walls are finished with a faux marble texture in a pale terra

cotta color. The recessed niches are equipped with glass shelves that support the imported Italian packaged delicacies. Terra Cotta "bricks" accentuate the self illuminated niches.

At the far end of the long and narrow space is a plastic laminate faced refrigerated case—also in terra cotta—and a service counter where orders are placed and drinks and desserts are picked up. A wave-like dropped ceiling floats directly over this area and helps to define it. The balance of the ceiling and the revealed HVAC equipment are painted a dark green.

The light aluminum and curved plywood chairs are pulled up to the honey beige laminate topped tables which are supported on black wrought iron bases. Uplights, dropped MR16 lamps and recessed incandescents combine with the light emanating from the niches to affect a relaxed and casual ambient glow.

DESIGN • TED Design & Associates, Inc. Richmond Hill, ON
INTERIOR DESIGN DIRECTOR • Peter K. H. Yip
PHOTOGRAPHY • Courtesy Peter Yip

Mad About Soup

The renovation of the 2500 sq. ft. store in West Hartford, CT by Judd Brown Designs called for quite a bit of planning. The client's desire was to have a small café sitting zone along with a service counter and a market sector for prepared foods—all on the ground floor space of an office building.

To create a "different" ambiance for this Northeast marketplace, JBD's design team opted for an eclectic sort of design and decor that leaned more towards a West Coast look. It would provide a welcome change. There is lots of light colored wood used in Mad About Soup. From the pale, timer laid floor and the curved service bar/counter that angles back along one wall to the light chairs and tables, the wainscot and the crown moldings—wood is in! Wood beams cross over the ceiling and a checkerboard of two colored woods highlights the ceiling area in front of the service counter. The color palette selected to go with the wood includes a hearty moss green, a rich terra cotta and a soft, creamy yellow-white. The same colors, in glazed tiles, are applied on the wall behind the counter and they are also used to accentuate the structural columns that rise up behind the beige, marble topped counter. The café seating can accommodate 20 self-servers and the tables are lined up along the wall opposite the focal counter. The tables are polyurethane finished natural wood and the chairs are covered in terra cotta and beige vinyl.

The lunch menu features gourmet sandwiches, soups, salads and assorted soft drinks. The dinner menu offers home meal replacement specialties.

DESIGN • JBD Judd Brown Designs, Warwick, RI

PROJECT MANAGER • Mark Palazio

INTERIOR DESIGN • Leah Wheary

GRAPHICS/ARTWORK & SOUP PLAQUES • Toucan Graphics

CUSTOM VEGETABLE VEILING PLAQUE • Foam Technology

PHOTOGRAPHY • Warren Jagger Photography, Inc.

Boston Chowda

The menu is simple and limited to soups and sandwiches with the emphasis on chowders and bisques as would benefit any take-out or stand-up-and-dine shop for soups in Boston or the New England area. What started out as a single store operation has quickly grown to eight outlets.

The client's desire, as stated to JBD, was "a simple, clean design" that would have the appeal and the character of a New England dockside seafood market. The result is fresh and clean but also warm and inviting and without any of the trite cliches one usually gets with seafood. The palette is neutral: white, off-white, toast, beige and brown complemented by a rich, orange-toned wood and satin stainless steel accents. The wood canopy that fans out over the service counter is filled with recessed spots and several dangling MR16 down lights. The service counter is faced with white marble framed with the same wood as the overhead canopy and the refrigerated food display case is finished in stainless steel. Glazed white 4x4 tiles cover the back wall of the kitchen/prep area and over it are the dark brown menu boards framed in nautical blue. The side walls of the shop are also finished with the same easy to clean and maintain tiles.

The floor is patterned with bands of beige and white mini tiles separated by borders of beige, toast and brown tiles. For those who can't wait to get home to indulge in the fresh soups and sandwiches there are several arced stand-up, marble topped tables resting on stainless steel legs.

The design is simple and has been planned so that it can readily be reproduced in a wide variety of potential market locations.

DESIGN • JBD Judd Brown Designs, Warwick, RI
DESIGN TEAM • Glenn Lepore/Mark Palazio/Leah Wheary
PHOTOGRAPHY • Warren Jagger Photography, Inc.

Souper Salad

The designers of the 5600 sq. ft. Souper Salad Express on Summer St. in Boston were influenced by diners and the streamline trains of the 1930s and 1940s as well as Fiestaware and Harlequin patterns that reflected the kitchen arts of that period. They used these influences to create the setting, shown here, that is targeted at the young adults working in the nearby office buildings.

To take advantage of the streamline theme, the designers at Morris Nathanson Design painted all of the existing brickwork semi-gloss white. "The crisp white look is sleek and sets the tone for efficiency." On this "blank" surface, the designers "painted" with lush, dense colors in an "eclectic contemporary" style and complemented it with tropical influences in artwork and graphics. The menu boards and signage are derived from old diner prototypes and the floor pattern was

styled after a 1940s rumpus room. According to the designers, "The Revival light fixtures are similar to those found at early drug store service counters." "We also introduced new contemporary wall sconces as our intention in the design was to be not so much literal in our detail but to express it in a contemporary fashion."

All surfaces had to not only be extremely durable but easy to maintain. All lower walls and counter fronts are finished in American Olean tiles in white, red and black. The counter tops are black avenite. Composite marble was used on the floors which are patterned with boxes within boxes in a play of black and red and accented with red squares. Like those found in early diners, the table tops are laminate with radial corners and ridged edges. Since the long, narrow space also had a high ceiling, the designers added a mezzanine for dining and the café can accommodate 50 diners.

The existing HVAC was retained and painted the same dark blue as the ceiling. To bring heating and cooling to the mezzanine an extension had to be added to the existing system. The pink and blue neon ribbons, the colorful tropical graphics and the shiny, corrugated metal accents all add up to a fun environment that is "retro" and "now" at the same time.

DESIGN • Morris Nathanson Designs, Pawtucket, RI
PRESIDENT • Morris Nathanson
VP • Peter Niemitz
VP/DIRECTOR OF DESIGN • Blase Gallo
DESIGNER • David Jackson
PHOTOGRAPHY • Warren Jagger Photography, Inc.

MEZZANINE FLOOR PLAN

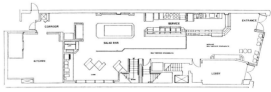

FIRST FLOOR PLAN

Seven on State Café

The seventh floor of the landmark Marshall Field department store on State St. in Chicago is devoted to food: food to be eaten in the store or purchased to-go for future use or as gifts. Walker Group/CNI of New York was challenged to renovate the outdated floor and create a state-of-the-art, interactive food and beverage facility that also included a food retail area.

To accomplish the task, the designers focused on the "theatrical nature of preparing food" and created five individual food stations with innovative, open kitchen areas. Here the diner can enjoy the show of watching the ingredients being mixed, the food being prepared and also become involved with the different equipment and techniques used by the master chefs. This is combined with a series of related facilities that allow customers to sample various foods as well as purchase the ingredients.

Not only did the architects/designers open up the atrium which had in the past been closed off, but they also re-opened the exterior windows so that diners can now not only enjoy watching the changing Chicago weather but also admire the unique skyline that is a visual record of architecture of the twentieth century. The new design is contemporary and clean and quite neutral in color and it is also very compatible with the rich, classical architecture of the central atrium.

The Walker Group/CNI design team specified a rich palette of mosaic tiles, cerrused woods and woven metals that are integrated throughout the floor. Curved walls that sweep in and out "create a dynamic background for the food prepa-

ration" while niches, cut into the walls, are used to decoratively display the "ingredients" and the "tools" of the culinary trade. Of special interest are the pendant lighting fixtures made of assorted silvery cooking equipment that hang over the main, light wood faced counter/bar. Each area or station is accentuated by backlit, dimensional letters that spell out the specialty. There are graphics as well that adorn the fascia over the openings into the kitchen.

In addition, the designers developed the logo, the menu boards, way-finding signage and the take-out packaging.

DESIGN • Walker Group/CNI, New York, NY

DESIGN PRINCIPAL • Jay Valgora

DESIGN TEAM • Alan Ademac, RA/Steven Kitezh/Marcyle Wakllman/Donald West

FOR DAYTON HUDSON

    DIR. OF STORE PLANNING • Jane Van Alken

    STAFF ARCHITECT • Michael Tietz

    DIR. OF VISUAL MERCHANDISING • Jamie Becker

    PHOTOGRAPHY • Susan Kezon

Nordstrom's In-House Café & Coffee Bar

FRISCO, TX

The 1200 sq. ft. café is located in the Nordstrom department store in the Stone Briar Mall in Frisco, TX. It represents a new dining concept for the noted retailer. The Café features a quick, "grab-and-go" connection to in-house prepared food and beverages as well as signature packaged food items in a stylish and visually inviting setting. The Engstrom Design Group of San Rafael, CA developed the interior design elements, the architectural layout and the finishes for this prototype design.

This new layout is only about one third of the size of a typical Nordstrom Café. The In-House Café & Coffee Bar is situated near the main entrance to the store—adjacent to the mall—in the space previously held by the Espresso Bar. John Clem, chairman of the restaurant division of Nordstrom sees this new concept as "a rest stop on the freeway leading to the store."

Inside bright colors, whimsical graphics, three dimensional interior elements and an efficient layout engage the visitor and also quickly points up what is available—and where. The lively café interior offers face-to-face service for coffee drinks, smoothies, sandwiches, salads and there is even a tempting children's menu. "In-House is the customer's first view of Nordstrom. The interior elements create a stylish yet timeless backdrop for the colorful and engaging graphics," says Jennifer Johanson, AIA, principal at EDG. "The layout, in

combination with the graphics, is intended to orient and direct the customer." Earth colors such as terra cotta, beige, and cream plus natural woods dominate the color/material palette. Mosaic tiles in red, orange and camel are used as accents to highlight the two-toned, wood veneered service bar/counter.

In the same space food related retail goods are presented on combined displayer/self service units and EDG also designed a system of millwork boxes to accommodate different products and offer a variety of display options. A nice add-on is the computer terminal with Internet access for customers who want to check their e-mail or shop at Nordstrom.com.

DESIGN • EDG Engstrom Design Group, San Rafael, CA
GRAPHICS • Duffy's, Minneapolis, MN
PHOTOGRAPHY • Richard Klein, Dallas, TX

Daisy & Tom Café

LONDON, UK

Dalziel & Pow, the London based design firm, created a child's dream of heaven here on earth when they designed the two story high, children's toy, game and book store on Kings Road in London. Daisy & Tom is filled with fun and fantasy—with a doll-scaled carousel—with nooks and crannies filled with wonderful things and a special café just for the children. Designed with utter simplicity and in a bold palette of red, blue and white, the Café offers special booth seating for the children in a scaled down choo-choo train that seems to be chugging down the red tiled floor. The walls and ceiling are white and the upholstery on the booth seating and the laminate table tops is a rich ultramarine blue. Red metal beams—part of the building's original construction—and some of the old brickwork are emphasized to add to the train depot ambiance. Brass accents on the train are complemented by the shiny brass trim on the benches along the wall and on the lighting fixtures as well.

There is an interactive quality to the scheme with make-believe drums and mechanisms with handles and levers for the children to play engineer or track switcher.

An open kitchen dominates one corner of the space and it is surrounded on two sides by dark tambour wood facing. The

vertical slatting is occasionally interrupted by a panel of horizontal strips outlined in copper. Brass shines on the foot rail on the floor. The original construction beams are painted red and create a dynamic presence in the kitchen along with the satin silver finished drop lights that also further the train station imagery. Signs, hung throughout as directionals, signify the various "stations" within the café.

DESIGN • Dalziel & Pow, London, UK

PHOTOGRAPHY • Courtesy of the design firm

Monopoly Coffee Bar

If the giant wood horse rising up three stories high in The Forum in Las Vegas doesn't get your attention, and if the crowds jamming in and around the colossus with the animated action behind the opening and closing doors doesn't whet your appetite—maybe you don't belong in The Forum and FAO Schwarz's dynamic store design isn't your cup of tea.

Once inside the oversized and overscaled store designed by AAD of Scottsdale, AZ and J. Newbold & Associates of New York, NY, it is all gapes and gasps as the wonders of childhood envelop you. One of the extra nice touches is the Monopoly Café on the upper level, in the games area, where the designers have

taken the world popular game blown it up to bigger-than-life proportions and given it a whole new spin. Though the toy store is all about children, the Café/Coffee Bar is OK for the more sophisticated tikes but it is really a respite for the parents or the weary grandparents.

The floor is decorated like a giant Monopoly board except the boxes that usually frame the field are now on the wall as a decorative frieze. The old familiar symbols are all there and they give the patron a retro-rush moment back to the good old days. Suspended over the squares are the "draw" cards and they have new quotes that are a bit more sophisticated than the original and also make references to the coffee stop. Even the little wood houses you "buy" are amusingly clustered here.

The designers stayed true to the Monopoly game source by using a palette of red, black and white with accents of green, orange and yellow. The familiar logo, set into the floor, greets patrons to the café.

In another area, the designers created a more space age soda bar with a Star Wars theme for the young ones. Animated figures—aliens, of course—entertain the lucky patrons seated at the bar and facing the arch shaped stage upon which the ETs are performing. Other space-y figures stand guard at the entrance to this cool blue, out-of-this-world setting.

DESIGN • AAD, Scottsdale, AZ and
J. Newbold & Associates, New York, NY
PHOTOGRAPHY • Courtesy of FAO Schwarz

Le Gourmet Café

Le Gourmet is an upscaled delicatessen/gourmet café located in the very chic Jockey Plaza Shopping Center in Lima. Designed by Jose Orrega Herrera of Metropolis, it is a café, a bar and an exhibition hall, all in one.

The architect/designer had a very cosmopolitan and European concept in mind when he designed this elegant space with large windows that open onto the main aisle of the mall. The red granite walls with the raised brass letters tell the story and the sidewalk café effect of the light, black metal chairs and tables set out in front suggest Paris in the spring or Rome anytime of the year.

The rich materials carry over into the interior with the verde gris marble trimmed service/display counter that angles back into the space. The same marble is used on the bases of the faux marble painted columns. Marble tiles follow the zig

zag pattern of the counter with the food displayed in the illuminated cases. Snacks and pre-packaged foods are displayed on built in shelves behind the counter. Seating is on the wood laid floor. Several tall, stand-up marble topped tables line the counter area. In the rear of the space–away from the windows—the feeling becomes more intimate and secluded: more café and less delicatessen. The recessed spots in the ceiling together with the lamps that pinpoint the changing exhibit of artwork on the walls create a soft, gentle glow of light here.

"The scale of the space and the use of warm materials make for a delicious and stylish environment," says Sr. Orrego.

DESIGN • Metropolis, Lima, Peru
ARCHITECT/DESIGNER • Jose A. Orrego Herrera
PHOTOGRAPHY • Courtesy of the designer

Segafredo

Fitch researched the Japanese market to identify those aspects of the Italian culture that would be most appropriate to integrate into the design of this new endeavor. "The overall brand image had to reinforce firstly its essential Italian characteristics and secondly the uniqueness of Italian espresso coffee." The new Espresso Café on the street level is very casual in feeling and the consumer has the choice of a wide range of Italian snacks as well as coffee machines, mini-espresso pots and other typically Italian coffee related products. In addition there is a self-serve system for speed and the convenience of those who want the quick stimulation of an espresso without taking the time out to linger over it.

Red is the color of choice here and the main serving counter/bar sparkles with the thousands of red glass mosaic tiles set in the front of the granite topped bar. The hot glow continues on the rear wall which carries the Segafredo logo and the espresso machines beneath it. There are some stand-up tables for the quick sippers and a curved bar on the rear wall seats others on tall stools.

The 5500 sq. ft. café designed by Fitch of London for the Sumisho Gourmet Coffee Co. of Japan is split over two levels and can accommodate over 100 patrons. Segafredo is the first joint effort of the supplier/retailer of Italian espresso, Segafredo, and the Sumitomo Group to create an Italian Espresso Café in Japan. With the expansion of tourist travel to Europe, the Japanese consumer has become more sophisticated and more open to alternative styles of coffee drinks.

Up on the second level it is time to relax. It is time out to sip and savor and be served. Red accent walls highlight the space as well as artwork and photography which has been provided by Fitch. They enhance the modern Italian style tables and chairs and the decor in general. Red topped tables are joined by contoured orange/red wood chairs and the light parquet wood floor gleams with a high sheen. Recessed lamps and Italian blown glass lamps provide the ambient light.

DESIGN • Fitch, London, UK

SENIOR EXECUTIVE VP/PROJECT LEADER •
  Giles Marking

SENIOR INTERIORS • Nick Butcher

SENIOR INTERIORS • Nadeem Moghul

PHOTOGRAPHY • Hiroaki Tadokoro

Surf City Coffee Company

SOQUEL, CA

Surf City Coffee Co. is a "love child." It is part of a love story between Dan Mc Court and his wife Suzanne and their pleasure in surfing. They also wanted to create a local coffee house which would supplement their incomes and provide Suzanne with the opportunity to do "something artistic, fun, friendly and flexible." "I am also very much entrenched as a local artist," says Suzanne McCourt, "and I wanted to bring that creativity and color to our store for others to enjoy."

The success of their first store, in Aptos, which was a remodel of an existing store led to this new space in Soquel. Since this is a new structure, the owners, working with Robert Palmer, an architect, and Tamara Harmon, an interior designer, were able to solve some of the spacial problems that were inherent in the Aptos shop. The result, shown here, is a spacious curvilinear structure filled with warm woods and fresh colors that blend an upscale feeling with artistic flair and the fun and free feeling of surfing. There is

outdoor seating on the pebble paved patio and a pair of doors open into the café.

The interior is sand and sun and Suzanne's artistic efforts are reflected in the waves sandblasted onto the sconce lighting as well as the designs on the laminated table tops. The sunny yellow/beige stucco walls of the exterior reappears on the interior where it is teamed up with blue, orange, and while mosaic tile accents set into the light beige floor and the bases under the gentle, light wood veneered counters and cabinets. Adding to the warm and friendly ambiance are the wood rafters that support the red tiled roof and the accents of the black metal legs on the contoured wood chair seats and backs. An artistically decorated surfboard floats across the sweeping fascia that separates the counter service area from the seating area beyond. The surfboard is like a dimensional logo. Water colors by Suzanne McCourt grace and accentuate the yellow/gold walls.

Each and every element that went into the Soquel Café was created by Suzanne McCourt and Tamara Harmon, the interior designer. This new operation, like the first one, has become an integral part of the community. Locals and tourists can stop for coffee or espresso drinks or the Surf City special milkshake for adults—the Surfaccino. Also available are pies, cakes, pastries and assorted light lunch options. On sale, in the store, are company logoed items such as mugs, T-shirts, sweat shirts and coffee related items. "Surf's up and the coffee is hot at Surf City Coffee Company"—and everybody is welcome.

OWNERS/DESIGNERS • Suzanne & Dan McCourt

INTERIOR DESIGN • Tarama Harmon of TH Designs, Pacifica, CA

ARCHITECT • Robert Palmer, AIA, Capitola, CA

PHOTOGRAPHGY • Peter Malinowski, Santa Barbara, CA

Plantation Coffee & Tea Company

The client wanted the new café to be "warm, dark, and open" and also incorporate the view from the windows on three sides of the space. He also wanted areas for group seating as well as more intimate seating. Pat Candeloro of Candeloro Designs was challenged by the 2000 sq. ft. space with its 20 ft. high ceiling. How to fit in a kitchen, a large service counter, 40 seats and still create "an open and airy space"? With essentially only one real wall to work with—the others are windowed—the main counter was designed as a kiosk in the center of the space. The circular design maximized the counter space for the required material and food display and the seating areas were arranged around this focal element. Each seating zone appears more intimate yet the spaces between make it look open.

Since the client preferred an "aged" look to the clean and contemporary feeling many favor in cafés, the "Greek" distressed murals set the look for the café. They also give the space a one-of-a-kind atmosphere. Hard modern surfaces were used only where the traffic was heavy and maintenance was required. The colors that were used reflect on the main prod-

uct offering—coffee. With the exception of the countertops, all the materials used were organic. The material palette included rich stained maple wood, honey colored stucco and dark stone tiles—"to give the space a very warm and appetizing environment." Much of the detailing was concentrated on the walls and the custom millwork. Multiple heavy bullnose trims were incorporated to relate back to the circular bench and counter.

For seating, Candeloro selected several different styles of chairs and couches. The different chairs were upholstered in assorted colored fabrics so that each area of the café picked up an individual flavor or character. The benches were custom designed to serve for banquet seating and patrons are quite comfortable on the large sofas that were installed.

Since the ceiling is so high, it was painted black and the lighting was designed on angled iron posts projecting out from the walls and the fascias. The light fixtures were enclosed with multi-colored glass lenses and at night they seem to float in the ceiling. All the ambient light are MR16s and they are on dimmers so the light level can be adjusted depending upon the daylight coming in through the windows.

DESIGN • Candeloro Designs, Concord, ON
PRINCIPAL • Pat Candeloro
PHOTOGRAPHY • Courtesy of the Designer

Tinderbox Espresso Emporium

GLASGOW & LONDON, UK

According to the owners of Tinderbox Espresso Emporium, Mathew Algie—a producer of coffee and branding ideas for retailers—Tinderbox was created "to form part of the social fabric of the 'urban villages' of Byres Road in Glasgow and Islington in London." The design, by Graven Images, is contemporary in spirit and in keeping with the image and attitude of its young adult patrons, but the designers have incorporated materials into the settings such as Vitrolite, Bakelite, Formica and vinyl that relate to the "golden age" of espresso bars—the 1950s. However, they used the materials, textures and colors with imagination, flair and sophistication to better play up the old/new, yin/yang aspect of the design.

The Glasgow store was the first one designed by Graven Images for Tinderbox Espresso. The interior also suggests a basement rec room of the 1950s—or a garage with the wood sheathed walls, the dropped ceiling, the simple black naughahyde upholstered benches to either side of the boat shaped Formica topped tables. The old leather, reclining airplane seats are the choice seats and they complement the black and maroon pillows on the bench seating. In the midst of all the contemporary design the amusing "old" materials are fun.

The London store which is more recent, is quite open and it replays the black, white and maroon colors along with the natural woods and the stainless trim. There is a built-in count-

er with pull-out stools as well as a "street watching" counter of stainless steel that crosses the steel framed Tinderbox window. Black and white marlite serves as a base for the white counter and as inset strips in the wood floor.

Tinderbox is not just an espresso bar/coffee shop. It is a "third place" where people can come and enjoy the very best coffee, find friends, read a magazine, listen to music or just "hang out." "It is a place of individuality, has a sense of fun—and has great coffee." It expresses the espresso lifestyle.

DESIGN • Graven Images, Glasgow, Scotland
DESIGN TEAM • Janice Kirkpatrick/Ross Hunter/Kirsty Lang
OPERATOR • Carlo Ventisei for Matthew Algie
PHOTOGRAPHERS • Keith Hunter (Glasgow),
  Niall Clutton (London)

Torrefazione Italia

Why would anyone want to open still another coffee bar/café in Seattle—the home of coffee bars and cafes? The new design created by GGLO of Seattle for Torrefazione Italia offers a very valid reason for trying the new place in town. As the name implies, this café exudes "the warmth of Italy" and the design captures the essence of a street-side Italian café—but updated.

Though the concept is traditional, the design is contemporary. The designers approached the design from the coffee counter as the focal point. The 15 ft. long curved bar is all mahogany and marble and exudes the richness of the coffee products offered. The espresso machine is "strategically located to create interaction between customer and barista." The old world custom of food plates displayed atop the counter is also introduced and that further advances the warm, traditional

quality of the design. Handcrafted, recessed casework is combined with wheat yellow to ocher colored walls and a slate blue dropped curved ceiling hangs over the bar to counterpoint the carefully selected artwork—actually a rotating exhibit of black and white photography—and the contemporary light fixtures. The quarry tile floor is composed of a range of soft, muted earth tones.

There are assorted seating options: from the blue striped upholstered banquette that hugs the pale yellow wall to the light oak chairs that pull up to the small tables with light wood tops. There are European style café settees facing each other on an area rug in front of glazed doors.

The display of Deruda pottery in the wall cabinets reinforces not only the Italian tradition but the inspiration for the colors used in the café. Even the live plants are set into Deruda urns. In the center of the space is a large table laden with plates and cups, fresh flowers and packed to-go coffee.

DESIGN • GGLO, Seattle, WA
PRINCIPAL IN CHARGE • Bill Gaylord
PROJECT MANAGER • Dave Heinen
PROJECT ARCHITECT • Todd Bertelloti
INTERIOR DESIGNER • Colleen Knowles
STAFF ARCHITECT • Wendy Chang
PHOTOGRAPHY • Peter Eckert, Eckert & Eckert, Portland, OR

Frisch's Big Boy

Big Boy family-style restaurants have been satisfying hungry people-on-the-go for a long time, but it was time to update the look and open up Big Boy to a whole new group of customers. The new prototype, in Batavia, OH, was designed by FRCH Worldwide Design based in Cincinnati. The designers based this design on consumer insights gained from extensive research. "The combination of food, music, decor and service all play a part in how the customer enjoys their dining experience."

"Frich's will always have a nostalgic aspect; the old memories will aid in the creation of new ones." It is still the same Big Boy with the same "home cooking" but it is being presented in a more updated setting. The new design went hand in hand with the redesign of the logo, the uniforms and all of the graphic elements. Outside, the glass block tower serves

both as the restaurant's front door and as a beacon to draw diners to this established, family-style dining establishment. A computer driven lighting systems allows the tower to be illuminated in a variety of changing colors at night or can be reset for colors to go with specific holidays or seasons.

Inside, the counter seats with the view into the kitchen is gone, and diners now have several seating options. The layout provides for a café area and a more traditional dining room. The café caters to smaller parties and family groups and the round tables and comfortable light colored bent plywood chairs create a cozy and intimate feeling on the multi-colored tiled floor. Curving partitions of the same tile separate this area from the serving counters. Overhead the lighting is hidden between the undulating wood beams that fill in the cut-out circle in the ceiling. The more traditional dining room is separated from the café by a light wood partition topped with a translucent plastic panel and the diner steps from the tiled floor onto a carpeted one. Here seating is on wood chairs and tables that can easily be rearranged to suit larger parties. Wood slat blinds, hanging globe lights and the use of natural wood all help to recall an earlier era.

The breakfast/lunch buffet that was always a popular Big Boy feature still exists but now it is against a wall. The new kitchen has three cook lines in order to move the drive-through line faster since the "drive-thru" makes up 30% of the company's business. According to Karen Maier, VP of Marketing for Frisch's, "We have created a relaxed atmosphere that is brighter and fresher where customers can feel comfortable eating alone or bringing their whole family out to dinner."

DESIGN: FRCH Worldwide Design, Cincinnati, OH
DESIGN TEAM:
   Thomas Horowitz: Principal-in-charge
   Steve McGowan: VP/Creative Leader
   Tessa Westermeyer: VP/Communications Leader
   Rebecca Stillpass: Brand Consulting
   Mason Proudfoot: Project Manager
   Bill Bily: Project Design Architect
   Jennifer Kerr: Graphic Designer
   Larissa Thayer: Visual Merchandising
FOR FRISCH'S BIG BOY
   Craig Maier: CEO
   John Hunter: VP/Property Development
   Karen Maier: VP Marketing

Arby's Big Sky

For some time Arby's has been known as THE roast beef sandwich headquarters in the field of fast foods. With this new "Big Sky" store in Colonial Heights, VA, Arby's creates an entirely new and more upscale image. Much of the new image is due to the design by Lawson Design of Annapolis, MD.

The interior design focuses on the Northwest (think Montana and Alaska) and on the great out-of-doors in general. The building itself is constructed of pink stone with red metal trim around the large windows. Highlighting the interior is the exposed wood truss ceiling with its custom art steel brackets. To create the desired atmosphere there is an authentic, 14 ft. tall Northwestern Indian totem pole and a two-sided stone fireplace with specially designed and fabricated artistic fireplace screens that separate the dining area from the serving lines. Other decorative focal elements are the metal sculptures of a standing grizzly bear and the heads of a moose and a deer.

There are four food areas and each has a unique counter design and signage to match. Arby's Gourmet version of its original menu is presented behind a mahogany and red marble faced counter. Here the back walls are covered with eight in. squares of apricot colored tiles. Tumbled marble designs on the rear wall and the counter front distinguish the Nito Burrito service counter. Here a patron can also watch an authentic Mexican tortilla making machine in action. White glazed tiles and a white marble topped, white tile faced counter defines Polo Pronto—the rotisserie chicken pod. The frozen custard stand has a brightly colored, hand cut, mosaic faced counter with a glass counter top. All the self-service counters

are accented with Tennessee brownstone and etched glass. The marble floors are accented with tumbled marble outline designs while a sharp colored wool Axminster carpet is used to simulate area rugs.

Mission style, stained glass lamps are suspended from the ceiling and attached to the partition walls. In addition to the contemporary artifacts in the dining area there are carnival style banners with quotes from Roy Rogers to add a feeling of authenticity.

DESIGN • Lawson Design Corp., Annapolis, MD
George Lawson & Kendyl Lawson
PHOTOGRAPHY • Hi-Tech Photos, Inc. Falls Church, VA

McDonald's

The design inspiration for this McDonald's in Darien, IL was derived from the Chicago school of architecture and the Prairie style. This, the second new architectural identity designed for McDonald's by Gensler, in its conservative box form fits "more appropriately and comfortably into its native environment" and "the new design also freshens and enriches the overall customer experience in new and consistent ways."

The "glass box" design presents the customer with a glowing, visible expression of the McDonald operation. The golden arches icon is paired up with one of a series of images that epitomize the brand. "The interior layout and plan of the restaurant reflects the extended effort to create unique, consistent, and intuitive experiences that cue the customer and crew

person quickly and easily." A low red wall separates the beverage bar and counter/customer service from the comfortable seating. "Two tops with scones emphasize a personal dining experience." Warm toned finishes and materials, wood chairs, pendant light fixtures and varying lighting levels create a warm, friendly ambiance and the consistent use of materials, colors and graphic elements helps to make this a comfortable and easily understood space. The Prairie tradition is restated in the colors, textures and materials used.

In the dining area the booths are framed with wooden drop soffits to provide views to the outside. Two-tops provide optional seating. Graphics and brand imagery are contained throughout. The "art rail" supports a series of brand snapshots featuring packaging, signage, Ronald's shoes and Speedee. "The images were created as a family, providing a choice for the owner-operators." The Big Mac brand image features tiny, dimensional golden arches that reinforce the brand message in a subtle but playful manner.

The new large-scale use of the Golden Arches applied to the front of the building facade "creates a strong, fresh application of brand that communicates a new perspective." Throughout the restaurant, Gensler used every opportunity to further promote the McDonald identity.

DESIGN • Gensler & Associates, San Francisco, CA

PHOTOGRAPHY • Courtesy of McDonald's

Bembos

CAMINOS DEL INCA, LIMA, PERU

and the "Americanized"—the color scheme of primary colors reaches out and grabs the would-be customer. The facade features yellow canopies, metal framework, and exposed areas of concrete, terrazzo and glass. The broken plane, the sharp angles, the triangular forms all break up the bulk of the building's architecture and helps to create the unique look one has come to expect of a Bembo restaurant. The architect/designer, Jose Orrego Herrera, is noted in Peru for his exciting and unorthodox architectural designs and he has established this one-of-a-kind look for the Bembo chain. Inside, that same excitement continues as the palette of red, yellow and blue is played out in infinite patterns and arrangements. The patron almost feels as though he or she has walked into a dimensional Mondrian painting or become part of a Dubuffet sculpture.

The circular, half-round and triangular shaped window areas detract from the straight lines of the architecture while accents of chrome yellow break out from the almost red ambiance. The white floors and table tops and the black metal accents on the light, loose table bases and chairs all add sharp contrasts. The rich, ultramarine blue appears on focal walls and in patterns on the yellow walls. Red and blue neon add sizzle and dazzle to the space as well. The red supporting columns, ringed in neon, add strong vertical accents to the overall design scheme.

DESIGN • Metropolis, Lima Peru
    Jose A. Orrego Herrera
PHOTOGRAPHY • Courtesy of the Architect

B embos is to Lima what McDonald's is to any major city in the U.S.—or the world. It is THE place for hamburgers, fries and soft drinks—for fast foods delivered fast and fresh. This new Bembos is located in the prestigious shopping center, Caminos Del Inca, in a residential part of Lima. The fast food operation is in a two story building and the service counter, kitchen and seating are located at street level and there is a more intimate dining area on the mezzanine.

The Bembos image and attitude is bright, sharp and in-your-eye. With its targeted market—the young, the trendy

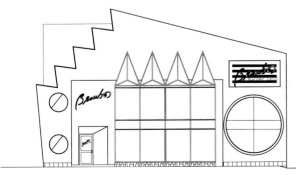

ELEVACION LATERAL

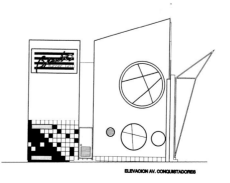

ELEVACION AV. CONQUISTADORES

In the large dining area, on the ground level, the red topped tables are patterned with black and the silvery chrome chairs are upholstered with red naughahyde. The boxed off, white floor is highlighted with gray terrazzo squares and an additional beverage bar, in a corner, is distinguished by the red, blue and yellow bar front. Paintings by local artists stand out from the rich, yellow gold walls.

The mezzanine is reached by an open staircase and the low ceiling adds to the feeling of intimacy—and quiet. There are red upholstered booths near the windows and loose table seating which is also finished in red. The window treatment plays up the assorted shapes and forms that are repeated on the walls.

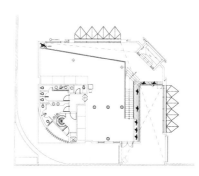

MOS Burger

Hamburgers may not be the most readily selected fast food for the older generation of Japanese citizens but it certainly has gained great popularity with the younger generations. MOS Burger challenged Design Forum to create a distinctive retail setting which would easily distinguish them from the encroaching McDonald's and reflect the "all organic product" as a quality and healthy alternative.

The MOS philosophy (Mountain-Ocean-Sun) is an all natural philosophy and it sees food as a "spiritual and artistic expression to be enjoyed." To carry through the message that a MOS burger is not just a hamburger, Bruce Dybvad, senior VP of Design & Architecture for Design Forum said, "We wanted to reject traditional fast food looks, therefore, there are no menu boards, no plastic laminates in the interior and nothing is back lit." Instead of the bright and often strong colors usually associated with fast foods, here the designers selected a gentle, muted palette.

Best Burger In Sangenjaya

Meals with fresh appeal.

A cloud filled sky, painted by a Japanese artist, spreads across the ceiling and gives the feeling of being out of doors. It also complements the articulated wall theme that suggests, symbolically, the mountains that are part of the MOS name. Most of the colors on the walls, table tops and upholstery have an almost California-casual look. "Japanese people really relate to the American sense of casual surroundings" and thus stone, rocks, wood and faux painting punctuate the space to create an "all natural" ambiance.

Throughout, the designers used English instead of Japanese for the signage and such. According to Bruce Dybvad, "English in Japan represents a more premium expectation in the consumer's mind." Using English gave MOS Burger a luster. The graphics and packaging, all designed by Design Forum, carry through the same colors and type as used in the shop. In addition to the "MOS Burger-ista"—the chef seen preparing the hamburgers in the open kitchen which can be viewed from the street as well as inside the store—there is the MOS Market. Here consumers can buy from a selection of organic vegetables, meats, sauces and breads. All of this along with seating along the walls on upholstered benches or pull up chairs or on stools at a floating counter is contained within 1000 sq. ft. of space on a heavily trafficked main street.

DESIGN • Design Forum, Dayton, OH
SR. VP OF DESIGN & ARCHITECTURE • Bruce Dybvad
GRAPHIC DESIGN • Dave Pinter
DIR. OF GRAPHIC DESIGN • Vivienne Padilla
PHOTOGRAPHY • Courtesy of Design Forum

Cajun Kitchen

From the exterior you would swear you were in Bayou country in Louisiana or somewhere just outside of New Orleans. However, you really are in Rolling Meadows, IL and getting ready to enjoy the Cajun treats being offered in the new Cajun Kitchen designed by the Aria Group of Chicago.

Raw, rough wood, stained corrugated metal sheeting, weathered shingles and wood—all aged and weather worn—go into creating the wayside and wayward look of Cajun Kitchen. The peaked gables and criss-crossing beams frame and accentuate the neon outlined signage. Set up, beneath the pitched corrugated roof, is an out-of-doors dining area for those who prefer to "rough it."

Inside the new restaurant/café/fast foods place—the dream-child of Lettuce Entertain You Enterprises (LEYE) and Popeye's Chicken & Bisquits—is rustic and just old-fashioned, down-country fun. The open-for-viewing kitchen is the big draw and the assorted foods are temptingly displayed under the red metal lamp shades, fitted with metal grid guards, that hang over the serve line. The relaxed, warm, and very inviting restaurant can seat 120 inside and about two dozen more on the porch.

The blacked-out ceiling and the dropped metal shaded lamps all contribute to the cozy, intimate ambiance which is enhanced by all the stained wood, the earth colored concrete floor and the 1950s diner touches such as the ribbed edges around the black laminate topped tables which are teamed up with "mismatched" black and yellow gold stained chairs. Pails and buckets and other old-fashioned kitchen equipment add to the atmosphere and the French Quarter signs and the memorabilia and artifacts enhance the "tradition and heritage" of the menu. House specialties include: roast beef and catfish Po' Boys; New Orleans style BBQ shrimp; BBQ Cajun ribs and two kinds of chicken—grille-roast which is Tabasco spiced—and Cajun fried chicken. If the food isn't "hot" enough diners can stop by the Sauce Bar and add some extra "fire" and spice. In addition there is a variety of cooling and quenching drinks—which can be necessary—and traditional New Orleans desserts.

Cajun Kitchen has proven popular with the young adults and family groups that find the moderate prices, the finger foods and the relaxed setting just right.

DESIGN • The Aria Group, Chicago, IL

PHOTOGRAPHY • Doug Snower

Potbelly Sandwich Works

A true story! A man owned an "antique store" and specialized in potbelly stoves, but business was slowing down and new "old" merchandise was getting harder to find. The enterprising shopkeeper started to sell sandwiches on the side to supplement his income. When his six in. sub sandwiches became so popular that he had to spend more time on the sandwiches than on his "antiques," he remodeled his store into a quick food restaurant and the surplus stock of his former business became the shop's decor.

This new store design by the Aria Group of Chicago reflects the history and tradition of the original store and today the ten different specialty subs are produced assembly-line style by the young, fresh-scrubbed De Paul University students who work there. In keeping with the feeling of the original 1977 store, there is a potbelly stove and the space is finished in rich, warm, earthy tones—lots of wood—and the quirky memorabilia that add extra flavor to the piled high subs, soups and the available drinks. Bryant Keil acquired the original store several years ago and under his aegis there are now four Potbelly Sandwich Works in Chicago and nearby Evanston.

In the Potbelly Works shown here, wood envelops the space: the wood floor, the mahogany stained counter, the wainscoting around the rear wall to line the intimate seating

areas, the paint peeling wood columns that support the mezzanine attic that is piled up with all sorts of artifacts, furniture, posters and clutter. The brick texture complements the woodwork and the natural beige floor tiles around the service counter. Period style globe chandeliers and pendant milk glass globe lights add to the ambient light as well as the atmosphere of the space. The bookcase filled with old books also serves to remind patrons that this was once an antique shop. This is not only a great place to behold—the food is great too.

DESIGN • The Aria Group, Chicago, IL
PHOTOGRAPHY • Doug Snower

C.V. Wrappers

Located in a restaurant food court in Columbus, OH is a new fast food concept that combines a wide variety of food ingredients and flavors in a new way. The project, as developed by Chute Gerdeman of Columbus, is wrapped around "a heroic, fictional, world-traveling explorer character named C.V. Wrappers." Using an environment inspired by a 1930s era air hangar/terminal, the designers tell the "story" of the hero in a series of comic book illustrations throughout the space and in the graphics. The graphics explain what the wraps are and the wraps are all tied in with cities—in keeping with the travel theme. Photos help the diners make their decisions.

Stainless steel and aluminum—including corrugated metals—help to make C.V. Wrappers' exterior stand out in the food court setting. The architecture is clean and "retro" with arches and columns and transom windows on the side. Added to the look are functioning hangar-like shutters and translucent glass panel doors. Patrons enter from the sides and exit through the front and once inside they may opt for sitting on stools along the bar/counter or sit outside on the "observation deck" which overlooks the mall. There are working view binoculars available on the deck for those who would like to scope the mall—or find their lost friends.

The 1930s atmosphere is emphasized inside the 1670 sq. ft. overall space in the sweeping curve of the counter which is faced with wood veneer and accented with bands of stainless steel. The countertops are stainless steel as well. The curve of the bar is restated in the bold line of the satin metal finished soffit above. The floors are finished with a matching dark wood and the walls in the prep area are covered with ceramic tiles. Just like the early airlines scheduled flights on a chalkboard, the menu is now written in chalk on a slate.

DESIGN • Chute Gerdeman, Columbus, OH
PHOTOGRAPHY • StudiOhio, Columbus, OH

Maui Tacos/Smoothie Island

ATLANTA, GA

Maui Tacos is a new concept in fast foods developed by Blimpie International. The idea was to move a successful "Fresh Hawaiian Mex" quick service restaurant originated in Maui to the mainland US and prepare it for roll-out. The Maui Tacos name had to be fully developed as a brand and The Retail Group of Seattle was commissioned to not only "brand" the concept but also conceptualize and realize an environment and presence that would attract diners.

According to The Retail Group, the Maui Tacos customer is looking for fresh, authentic tasting food in an environment that is relaxed and hip. It is not your "ordinary rice and beans joint." The designers leveraged the Hawaiian mystique in a casual, laid-back style using unexpected and vivid elements that go with the new tag line—"It's Mexican with Mauitude."

The 56 seat, 2100 sq. ft. space opened in Atlanta, GA and is finished in a "cross cultural" palette of creams, sands, and taupes combined with Hawaiian style florals and red, yellow and green that are used to represent the lush, tropical foliage. To create an "escapist aesthetic," the designers used a garage-like setting filled with retro Hawaiian imagery such as vintage photos, old posters, Hawaiian shirts and textiles, surfboards and souvenirs. The casual feeling is also reinforced by the "found objects" that fill the space such as the eclectic mix of mismatched chairs and tables. Old corrugated metal sheets clad some of the rough construction walls and they are painted with a "faded" mural of fruits and vegetables. Sprayed

---

DESIGN • The Retail Group, Seattle, WA

PROJECT MANAGER • Ernie Gilbert

CREATIVE DIRECTORS • Greg Arhart & Ashley Bogle

STORE PLANNER • Conrad Chin

GRAPHIC DESIGNER • Ivan Silantyev

PHOTOGRAPHY • J.Maris, Photographer

across the wall is the motto "Mexican with Mauitude." One of the really fun focal elements is the rusty old Volkswagen bus that seems to have crashed into the shop's interior. It is loaded down with crates and cartons, cans, jars and pre-packaged foods: a total grocery on-the-go. The Salsa Bar offers a wide selection of unusual salsas that can also be purchased to-go. The abundance of fresh fruits and vegetables communicates freshness and quality as well as adding to the visual brightness to the Maui-Mex fusion.

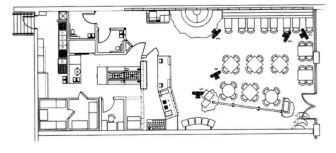

American Hot Dogs

What is more American than a "hot dog," and for those who are experts or have gourmet palates nothing is quite as good as the 100% kosher beef frankfurter. Situated in a mall in Caracas in Venezuela, American Hot Dogs caters this all-American favorite to those South Americans who have a yen for something that tastes of the USA. Served up with Hershey milkshakes and a variety of add-on toppings especially suited to the Venezuelan taste, this shop owned by Cesar Enerique Olivo and Adriana Perez Benatar and designed by Grid 3 International is a big hit!

Even though faced with a tight budget and the desire by the clients for a design that would become a marketing tool, Grid 3 came up with this prototype design which has already been rolled out in a dozen other locations. Red glass mosaic tile was used to create the distinctive and attention-getting red portico that has lights set in on both sides. With the exception of the stainless steel walls in the prep area, the other walls are tiled with small red squares. The flooring is cast marble and it complements the Carara marble table top, the stainless steel service counter and the chrome stools upholstered in zodiac burgundy naughahyde. They also recall the look of diners of the 1960s. Adding impact to the design of this tucked away fast food operation is the bold diagonal pattern of red and yellow tiles that lead the shopper to the service counter.

Of the 1500 sq. ft., 1000 sq.ft. is on the main level and it accommodates the kitchen and the eating area. The 500 sq. ft. mezzanine provides additional seating as well as space for public restrooms and a stock area.

DESIGN • Grid 3 International, New York, NY
PARTNER IN CHARGE • Marcelo Albertal
PHOTOGRAPHY • Marcelo Albertal

Donatos Pizza

The secret to Donatos success—and the Donato name is supreme in pizzas in Ohio—is in the recipe and the operation. Deemed "the best Pizza on the block," Donatos has decided to develop a new prototype environment to capitalize on its best features and to win over an even greater share of the market. Jim Grote, founder of the company, called upon Chute Gerdeman of Columbus for the new design perspective.

What the Chute Gerdeman design team attempted to capture in color, texture and design is the essence of "quality and personal friendly service." They have created in the 2480 sq. ft. space an atmosphere that suggests the pizza parlor when it was the neighborhood gathering place. Now, as then, patrons can enjoy the "theater" of watching the pizza making process. By placing the preparation area center stage, it becomes a more interactive dining experience. Items that one would expect to find in a family kitchen have been incorporated into the design scheme and emphasis has been placed on the "community connections" of Donatos with the neighborhood in which it is situated.

The brick facade is warm and inviting and the red, "raised eyebrow" awnings over the mullioned windows add a whimsical touch. The interior is filled with natural woods, warm and earthy colors, for example, the terra cotta ceramic tiles that frame the kitchen/prep area and the red topped Formica tables, banded in ribbed steel like the old fashioned diner tables of the 1950s and 1960s. Ever so subtly and respectfully there are also touches reminiscent of the family kitchen of the post WW ll era such as the counter and the chrome pull-up stools. The booth seating, along the window walls, are also upholstered in vinyls that recall the byegone era and the booths are illuminated by hanging, conical metal lamps. Throughout the floor is paved in creamy colored tiles.

A dining alcove, differentiated by the blue patterned carpet and separated by glass and wood doors, is set aside for groups or private parties. Here, the wall mural and the decorations are based on the new packaging designs created by Chute Gerdeman for Donatos. Using craft paper background and lots of red pepper red as the signature color, the pizza boxes and bags are covered with handwritten notes from Jim Grote, the founder, about the company as well as whimsical doodles and idle thoughts. It is this "personal tone-of-voice" that also carries through in the rest of the design.

Greenery and expert lighting make this a fast food place where one wants to hang out.

DESIGN • Chute Gerdeman, Columbus, OH

PRINCIPAL • Dennis C. Gerdeman

PROJECT MANAGER • Greg DeLong

BRAND POSITIONING • Lee Peterson

CREATIVE DIRECTOR OF ENVIRONMENTS • Maribeth Gatchalian

CREATIVE DIRECTOR OF GRAPHICS • Alan Jazak

GRAPHIC DESIGNER • Adam Limbach

GRAPHIC PRODUCTION • Susan Siewny

VISUAL MERCHANDISING • Joe Baer

PHOTOGRAPHY • StudiOhio, Columbus, OH

Sbarro's

For many New Yorkers the name Sbarro is synonymous with good Italian food in quick serve restaurants. The new design, as shown here, was introduced on Broadway and Canal St. in Manhattan—at the entrance to New Yotk City's famous Chinatown and Little Italy neighborhoods as well as the Wall St. area. The client requested that the 110-seat restaurant have the feeling of a "street café." In addition to selling pizza-by-the slice, Sbarro's wanted to also offer an expanded menu that would include buffet selections. The building itself is an historic, three story, Art Deco building and the front doors and trim are original. The 3400 sq.ft. ground level space has almost 12 ft. high ceilings and the existing pillars and beams made it desirable—from the designers point of view—to expose the ductwork and paint it out to

match the ceiling. The whole project was accomplished with simple gyp board and all the replastered areas were painted tomato red. The wainscoting below is hand set multicolored mosaic tiles capped with black tiles. The same cracked and crazed mosaic of broken tiles decorates the front of the service counter. To suggest the street café, the floors are laid with tiles set in assorted patterns to "showcase the columns and help define the food line."

The seating area is separated from the food line by dividers of overscaled perforated wood veneer laminates crowned with fluted glass panels. The patrons have a choice of seating; banquettes on wood laminate legs upholstered in red vinyl, booth seating with a checkerboard of red and ocher vinyl backs and seats, high top tables and chairs in light woods and pedestal tables with red laminate tops edged with ribbed aluminum trim and wood chairs with upholstered seats. The checkerboard of red and ocher vinyl appears on the rear wall under a colorful mural.

A focal point in the design is the brilliantly illuminated buffet table with its array of prepared foods. The red and ocher laminate finished base has stainless steel trim and the same shiny metal is used on the sneeze guard and tray rail to add to the flash and dash of the unit. Pendant bounce lights hang in front of the food line and the service counter to light up the food presentation and the preparation. On the existing columns overscaled alabaster lamps are hung. The custom murals are accentuated by exterior-type billboard lights while black track lighting illuminates the menu signage.

"The design was to reflect a carefree eating area where one could feel comfortable, sidewalk eating, an easy in and an easy out and accessible like a food court."

DESIGN • Morris Nathanson Design, Pawtucket, RI

PHOTOGRAPHY • Warren Jagger Photography, Inc.

Pasta Central

Pasta Central is another new concept for Blimpie International and they brought the idea to The Retail Group of Seattle to develop as a "brand" and as a retail operation. The concept is for a fast-food, eat-in or take-out Italian specialty store with fresh, high quality food prepared daily on the premises. The "branding" was to create a unique personality that quickly explained the concept. In creating the brand, the designers had to come up with visual cues which would identify the shop and the product as "fresh and fun" and that would appeal to the time-poor consumer in search of delicious food.

Using active yellows and greens for the signage on the exterior of Pasta Central gives the store a vital quality. Inside the designers used straightforward, simple materials and relied on color blocking and massing "to reflect the personality of Pasta Central." Using red, yellow blue and green as the major colors with accents of black and white, the design team affected a bright, sunny, amusing and animated interior. Black and white checkerboard pattern tiled floors and violet

lined cement flooring complement the dark green chairs and tables for those who prefer to eat-in. Natural wood seats and chair backs go with the wood dado/chair rail in the dining area. The Pasta Central images and colors combined on the billboard-like wall "reinforces the brand positioning as fun, convenient and value oriented."

There is an easy access refrigerated case which features a menu of home meal replacement items that can be for eat-in or take-out. All foods are assembled in the back area and consumers can therefore concentrate on the Pasta Central product offerings "while maintaining a clean, organized viewing point." All the signage and graphics are executed in bold colors within a Mondrian format that creates a fun and distinctive look.

DESIGN • The Retail Group, Seattle, WA
PHOTOGRAPHY • Courtesy of The Retail Group

Long John Silver's

T he new Long John Silver's prototype design, as created by Design Forum of Dayton, OH, incorporates a co-branding with A&W. Instead of the ramshackled, weather-beaten old shack/building that was the familiar facade of the old Long John Silver of yore, the new, up-dated facade—mostly white with accents of red, yellow and blue—features two towers that incorporate both the Long John Silver's and the A&W brands. The silvery metallic roof top is echoed in the awnings.

The primary goal, along with the new image, was to "re-establish the casual and fun, dine-in experience in an environment in which customers want to stay to enjoy a mea." The designers tried to distance the ordering

process in the layout from the usual fast food operation by separating the order station from the pick-up station. This redirects the focus from the kitchen area. For a color palette, the design team opted for "warmer and more appetizing" shades of marine blue, aqua, yellow and red. Throughout the nautical theme is uppermost; not only in the colors but in the wave-like pattern that is replayed in the upholstery of the booth seating. Creamy "waves" roll over blue bases with yellow piping as a highlighter. There is also a fish-themed wall-covering introduced on some of the walls along with decorative, seaside and water's edge murals. The creamy white table tops are complemented by the red and white tiled floor laid in a checkerboard pattern.

To emphasize Long John Silver's tradition as a "reputable and relevant quick service retailer," the designers added warm wood tones like on the beams that criss-cross overhead and the brass accents. Marine-style antique brass down lamps hang over some of the booths and the same metallic luster highlights the decorative sign holders between the booths.

Throughout the feeling is light and fresh as an ocean breeze or the fish being offered in the comfortable, friendly setting.

DESIGN • Design Forum, Dayton, OH
CHIEF CREATIVE OFFICER • Bill Chidley
DIRECTOR OF GRAPHICS • Vivienne Padilla
PHOTOGRAPHY • Jamie Padgett

Dai Bai Dang

Located in the Marketplace at River Park Mall in Fresno, is a new idea in Chinese dining created by Akar Studio of Santa Monica. For centuries Asians have dined at night food stands that fill the cities and towns when evening falls and markets are still open. Now it is possible to sample those foods—or at least similar foods—in the comfort of the 4200 sq.ft. Dai Bai Dang restaurant/café.

For Sat Garg, the principal of the design firm, creating the spirit of the night market for Dai Bai Dang was a challenge. "Open kitchens, bamboo market stand imagery, and a ceiling of backlit fabric reminiscent of the giant sails on Chinese junks in Hong Kong were used for cultural ambiance." The design team created "a kind of visual scrapbook" of Asian flavors which include the intricate use of volumes and shapes, movement in the ceiling elements, water-

colors and photographs on the walls and the overall relaxed lighting plan.

The need for a single traffic aisle with two-direction movement was solved by using tinted concrete embedded with stones, tile and brass floor markers that are etched with the names of the best night food markets in Asia. "We created a subtle Asian down-home feeling," says Sat Garg, "to attract clients." The textures are complemented by the colors of Asia: reds, rustic bronze, copper and natural woods. The "Asian Fusion" food concept that has been introduced with such flair has taken off and turned Dai Bai Dang into an exciting place to dine.

DESIGN • Akar Studio, Santa Monica, CA

PRINCIPAL IN CHARGE • Sat Garg

China Inn

To get away from the stereotypes of Chinese restaurants and especially those serving up fast foods in malls, Gilbert Chang of China Inn came to Sat Garg of Akar Studio in Santa Monica. To avoid the usual cliches, Garg stayed away from the red tiles and the bamboo that usually serves as design references for Chinese fast foods. Instead the design team mixed pale yellow walls with curves and asymmetrical ceiling planes. Added to this are clear veneer woodwork and green grained table tops that brighten up the space.

This China Inn is located in the upscale and outdoor Fashion Valley Center in downtown San Diego. To create a strong identity for this flagship store, Sat Garg designed an angled shopfront with a gleaming copper pediment entrance. The sweep of copper sheeting is angled forward over the off-centered entrance. The window is "broken" with slanted black metal strips and areas of colored glass add to the exciting, off kilter look of the facade. Floating on a curved horizontal plane are the dimensional letters that spell out the name.

Through the opening one can see the soft, muted tones of the interior and the swirling, flowing forms over the dining counter and the service counter. A unique light drops through the central ceiling well for dramatic impact. The designers met the client's goal by designing a new direction that employs stylish textured interiors with subtle colors and menu boards that are art. Throughout there is a focus on the small design details. The architect/designer wanted to create a strong presence by using the idea of yin and yang as interlocking forces. "It's a one of a kind," sums up Sat Garg.

DESIGN • Akar Studio, Santa Monica, CA
PRINCIPAL • Sat Garg

Manch Wok

From almost anywhere in the Scarborough Town Centre's food court the newly designed Manchu Wok stand is drawing attention. As designed by the Hirschberg Design Group of Toronto, it is the dimensional, custom crafted dragon that makes its presence felt and it is the big draw to the Manchu Wok concession. "He is serious, but friendly and his illuminated eyes are piercing but gentle." The designers maintained the standard colors associated with Manchu Wok but added a dark purple to give new impetus to the palette. Multi-colored glass tile inserts are randomly set into the purple ceramic tile backdrop to "add sparkle to the already dazzling design." Raised backlit panels are set to either side of the curved display case where the food is on view. The dragon's body and the display case are made of stained tambour which simulates the look of bamboo—to add a touch of Asian flair.

Manch Wok specializes in Chinese fast food ranging from Cantonese to Szechuan. It is one of Canada's largest fast food operations with almost 80 outlets in Canada.

DESIGN • Hirschberg Design Group, Toronto, ON
PHOTOGRAPHY • Interior Images, Toronto, ON

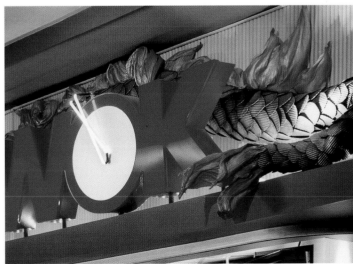

Marché

Marché is a concept that has set ripples going in how to design a food court or food service operation. The "whimsical and evocative" design for this Marché had to be fitted into the infrastructure of the Prudential Center in Boston and Bergmeyer Associates of Boston was commissioned to create the fit for the design originally conceived by Moncor Design Associates of Toronto.

Housed on three levels, the project is "a veritable feast for the palate." It combines elements of an outdoor European marketplace, a fine dining restaurant, and a sidewalk café. It is a multi-station food court with an international, cooked-to-order menu. Using fresh, locally grown foods and cooking in full view of the patrons—"The aromas and sounds of cooking along with the energy and bustle of a fresh street market, or marche, provide the entertainment."

The concept originated in Switzerland about 17years ago by the Movenpick Group and has been successfully translated throughout Europe, Canada, the Middle East and Asia. This is the American debut for the concept. In addition to the afore-mentioned dining options, there is "Caveau"—a wine bar that offers diners assorted wines and beers along with the lighter fare found in the Marché restaurants. Pre-prepared foods, meats, produce, wines, freshly baked breads and home-made chocolates are available at "Take Me! Marché¡"—a to-go operation, and "Marchelino" which also offers a limited menu of lunch and take-out items.

With the blacked out ceiling and a floor finished to look like worn slate—the illusion begins. Trees seem to grow up and leafy branches spread out to hide the pipes and vents that

DESIGN SUPERVISION/ARCHITECT • Bergmeyer Associates, Boston, MA

INTERIOR DESIGN • Moncor Design Associates, Toronto, ON

CLIENT • Jorg Reichert, Movenpick Restaurants, Toronto, ON

PHOTOGRAPHY • Lucy Chen Photography, Somerville, MA

run amok overhead. The individual food stands are full of color and personality and designed to suggest the cuisine of the country of origin. Old barrels, crates, pallets and hand carts as well as other rustic and provincial elements double as atmospheric props and as elevations, risers and containers for the fresh and pre-packaged foods to-go. Arcades of lights, multi-colored canvas awnings, bushels and baskets brimming over with fresh greens and fruits, ceramic tiles, provincial furniture and fabrics, brick-faced, wood burning ovens, flaming rotisseries, chalk board signs and hand scrawled specials add to the street market feeling of Marche.

Because of the unique Marche concept, Bergmeyer Associates needed to obtain many permits that are usually not part of the architect/designer's domain. Marche buys all of its foods locally and the produce is delivered fresh each day. They are not only used to decorate the baskets and bushels but they are the ingredients of the food being offered in Marche. Bergmeyer needed permits from the Board of Health, Inspectional Services Dept., Boston Development Authority and Boston Properties, the building landlord.

Foodlife

Foodlife, in the tradition of Marche, is an international food court located in the Watertower vertical mall on Michigan Ave. in Chicago. In a deep, dark and romantic glen setting dozens of different food stands offer a variety of global inspired flavors and tastes. In the original press kit for Foodlife the management said-"You have a social life, a business life, and a love life. Now then, there is an environment dedicated to your food life."

The spacious, sprawling food court has over a dozen different food stations and the stations change as people's tastes change. Some stands that were originally in the food court have yielded to newer influences such as the three concessions shown here that were designed by The Aria Group of Chicago. As wraps have grown in popularity over the standard sandwich or sub, Foodlife now boasts of a stand that dishes up creative, made-to-order, customized wraps. The corrugated metal counter and the fascia over the compact white tiled prep

area distinguish this stand from the antiques wood and canvas trimmed stands around it.

More upscaled and more "finished" than those surrounding them are the "Oases Noodles" and the "Pasta Fresca" concessions. The open kitchen of Noodles is framed with a sophisticated cherry wood facade of squares and the five hanging wok pans are pierced to spell out "Oases" while the "Noodles" is a yellow noodle strand of neon. The tray support is a slab of clear lucite that reflects the lights from above. The customer can select from the many ingredients displayed on the tilted white marble counter and have a customized wok dish prepared before his very eyes.

"Pasta Fresca" also has a wood facade/counter and the pseudo piers, to either side, are capped with white and yellow

ceramic tiles. The piers support a hammered copper arch that bears the stand's name as well as some of the freshly made noodles. Using a color palette of flour and eggs, a rich ocher yellow is combined with the white glazed tiles of the back wall of the prep area to enhance the presentation of the gold colored noodles. The rustic Italian feeling is carried through with the chalkboard signage and the black and white photos of "mama" making noodles.

DESIGN • The Aria Group, Chicago, IL

PHOTOGRAPHY • Mark Ballogg, Steinkamp/ Ballogg, Chicago, IL

Terminal Three Food Court

Though the traveler may be traveling in the 21st century, he can stop in at the Terminal Three food court at the Pearson International Airport in Toronto and find himself back in the a downtown neighborhood as it may have looked half a century ago. Hirshberg Design Group reconfigured the 5500 sq. ft. space into "an interactive, theatrical environment." They created a world within a world with fond memories of the past and an imagined multi-cultural neighborhood filled with fast foods such as Mrs. Vanelli's Italian Foods, Weber's Hamburgers, and Williamson's Coffee Pub. The many-layered and textured streetscape that houses these vendors also is home to some fictitious shops like Rosie's Flower Shop, Kosta's Fruit Stand and Mr. Lee's Grocery.

The color schemes and materials relate directly to each individual section of space. To reinforce the out-of-doors concept, natural tones were used like the floor tiles as "reflective of the elements they help establish". There are natural greens in the park and the city lanes and alleys are picked out in browns and charcoals. Painted wood siding, simulated sandstone, stucco and brick veneers are used to add depth and dimension to the "houses" and "store fronts" that line the food court. In addition to this and adding to the illusion there are focal elements sch as a newsstand booth for seating, a streetcar which also doubles as a sit-down dining area and it is great fun to look up at the illuminated windows over the shop fronts and spy on the "dwellers" in the apartments.

It is always nighttime in the food court. The ceiling has been blacked out and a carefully modulated lighting scheme was implemented. There is illumination from the lamp posts, from the shop windows and from the windows above as well as the patio lanterns and the store signs. The Terminal Three food court is a great place to people watch as well as while away some time while waiting for a flight.

DESIGN • Hirschberg Design Group, Toronto, ON

PHOTOGRAPHY • Interior Images, Toronto, ON

Best Fest Food Court

"Celebrating culture at every entrance, Concord Mills reminds visitors coming and going that they're immersed in a proud and well crafted North Carolina heritage." Designed by Kiku Obata & Co. of St. Louis, the Best Fest Food Court is one of the eight courtyards that serve the seven "neighborhoods" that make up the 1.4 million sq. ft. Concord Mills in Concord, NC.

From "the wacky to the wondrous to the whimsical to the wistful," the designers created a "visual vocabulary" that celebrates the many facets and wonders of North Carolina: crafts, festivals, nature, music, sports and traditions. According to Kevin Flynn, VP at Kiku Obata & Co., "The themed court-

yards at Concord Mills offer opportunities for shoppers to gather and chat." They become social gathering places and probably no area is as social and as much of a gathering place than the Best Fest food court. The design team developed a series of whimsical and wacky characters that fly wide, high and colorfully and cartoonishly handsome over the spacious food court. There is a pie-pecking chicken, a salamander playing a fiddle, and a pair of crabs—Cody Blue and Blue Skywalker—who perform warm-up exercises on the custom designed table tops.

Overhead Blue Crab Derby and Orville and Wilbur Bee pull a "What's The Buzz" banner across the space. These ten to 12 ft. high figures are fabricated of foam and sintra board. Also included in the menagerie of characters are Wenda and Wally Woolyworm showing their clogging techniques while a hog calling contest goes on nearby. Daffodil N. Bloom puts her "petals to the metal" to pass Peanut R. Goobers to win the Firehouse Race.

In addition to the array of colorful figures overhead there are multi-colored banners and carnival lights to add some glitter and pizzazz and the "fireworks" that effectively finish off the festive atmosphere.

DESIGN • Kiku Obata & Co., St. Louis, MO

PROJECT TEAM • Kiku Obata/Kevin Flynn, AIA/Dennis Hyland, AIA/Denise Fuehne/Jennifer Baldwin/Teresa Norton-Young/Gen Obata/Carole Jerome/Tom Kowalski/Nikki Hite/John Scheffel/Kathleen Robert/Jeff Rifkin

ARCHITECT • D'Agostino Izzoquirk Architects (DAIQ), Somerville, MA

PHOTOGRAPHY • Jon Miller, Heidrich Blessing Photography, Chicago, IL

Omni Diner

One of the features of the total design package of the 650,000 sq.ft. office building designed for Reckson Associates by Mojo Stumer Architects of Roslyn, NY is the Omni Diner on the main level of the building. The Diner was designed for the use of the executives and their support staffs who work in the building to be used as a cafeteria/lunchroom. Instead of the usual corporate dining facility, Mojo Stumer came up with the fun retro concept of doing their version of a 1950s diner.

The facade within the building looks like the old fashioned dining car with the art moderne striped metal decor, the curved roof and the glass block windows. The faux brick wall and the globe lights and the lamp post all refer to a byegone era. Within—though the space is big and airy—the archi-

tects/designers have played with all the usual icons to create a new look. Curved glass block walls sweep into the servery area with the black and white checkerboard floor executed in miniature square tiles. The "Thank You" on the floor is for those who are leaving.

The color scheme is out of the past as are the materials. Teal green and cherry red dominate with black and white played up in the accents. Red naughahyde upholsters booths line one wall which is resplendent in patterned panels of aluminum banded with a green and white border of mini tiles. The L-shaped dining counter has the familiar chrome diner stools with red seats banded with ribbed metal and the white Formica topped shelf/counter is also finished with the corrugated edging.

Neon ribbons outline the curve of the counter up on the dropped ceiling soffit and period style lamps with silvery reflector shades outline the sitting area. The raised ceiling, in the center, is tinted a cool, sky blue. As the diner leaves, a friendly aproned figure is there to say good-bye as the patron passes the neon outlined Coca Cola bottle. This design has been "a total success" and not only attracted the workers in the building but those from the neighboring office buildings.

DESIGN • Mojo Stumer Associates, Roslyn, NY

PHOTOGRAPHY • Frank Zimmerman/Andrew Appel & Marc Samu

Med Grill Café

Set between rich terra cotta colored marble walls and a seven story waterfall to one side and in the atrium that soars to a giant skylight overhead is Med Grill Café, an elegant, rich and refined self-service food court. The self-service area is set to one side of the space and a full service café/restaurant is on the other side in this design by Jack Baum of Tree House Designs of New York.

The food display counters are divided into two major zones. There is the quick service pastry and coffee station located at the foot of the escalators that descend from street level and a four part, full menu station where diners can have breakfast, lunch or dinner. In the full menu station, hot foods are kept warm on a state-of-the-art Corningware counter top which is finished in marble. The cold counters for sandwiches and salads are finished similarly and all have extended marble tray rails across their fronts. A cold beverage station stands next to the cashier's desk.

The materials used in the Med Grill Café were selected in keeping with the direction already set in the Trump Tower's mall interior architecture. Custom, hand selected Italian marble was matched to the existing marble and polished brass trim helps to blend the "old" with the "new." As a comple-

Med Grill

ment to the existing fixtures, the designer specified hand rubbed mahogany wood and Baum also designed custom light fixtures to "distinguish the Med Grill area from the other public spaces."

The previous restaurant was renovated with new furniture, new finishes and a liquor bar made of solid mahogany with a marble top and polished brass trim. A peach-tinted mirror frames the back bar. There is seating for 120 in the atrium space and 87 more can be served in the full service café.

DESIGN • Tree House Design, Ltd., New York, NY
PRINCIPAL • Julius S. "Jack" Baum
PHOTOGRAPHY • Stephen J,. Carr

Marketplace Café

The CNN Tower—the "world's tallest building"—has now also become the "world's tallest entertainment destination" with the completion of the Tower's revitalization and expansion. Guests can now discover the secrets of the CNN Tower through interactive, multi-media films and touch-screen exhibits as well as historical videos. In addition there are now specialty rides, game arcades, films, a Marketplace featuring authentic Canadian and First Nation arts and crafts, sporting merchandise and travel souvenirs.

It is here, at the base of the Tower, where the skywatchers who have ascended to the top and then descended find themselves in the Marketplace. That is where they will find the Marketplace Café. The café offers fresh market fare prepared at several different stations. Diners can choose from an array of foods ranging from pastas, oven baked pizzas, grilled meats, panini and wrap sandwiches and all are available in the super slick, super crisp, contemporary setting. Within a calm and coherent overall plan each food station is designed for maximum practicality. The Espresso/Cappuccino Bar is

highlighted by a maple and wood grid and has backlit glass fixtures while the Pizza station features butcher block and woven steel fixtures set against a multi colored mosaic background. The designers selected materials and finishes that are both contemporary and timeless in addition to being functional and durable, since there are as many as two million visitors annually.

Marmoleum surfaced aisles and fixtures that incorporate both open shelving and closed cabinets make the busy area efficient as well as attractive. The mar resistant, lightweight aluminum chairs make it feasible to rearrange the seating areas to accommodate large or small groups. The dining area also boasts of a rich backdrop of curved honeytree veneer wall panels with comfortable bench seating in front.

There is also a selection of packaged foods for the diners to take along and a carefully planned play of light draws their attention to the product display. The cash area features more displayed merchandise, concealed storage, dramatic backlit signage and ample queuing space.

DESIGN • ll X lV Design Associates, Toronto, ON
PHOTOGRAPHY • David Whittaker

Cosmic Diner

The Brantford Charity Casino is situated in a two story high building that was originally a Museum of Technology. As rehabbed and completely redesigned the upper level consists of four themed gaming areas but of special interest to us is the Cosmic Diner which is located at street level.

It doesn't quite look like any diner that may have existed in the 1950s or 1960s. It is more like one you might find at the end of a space trip to the next century. The space is light, bright and open. The tiled walls are patterned in ombred bands that range from soft gray and greige to almost white, while the floors are laid in giant squares of creamy beige tile. The same blond color feeling is carried over to the light chairs and tables set out on the floor: the chairs are bleached maple with steel frames and the table tops are off-white laminate edged with cherry wood. Highlighting the seating area are the ornamental railings of glass encased disks and swirling ribbons

of steel that wrap around the seating area and the suspended planet-like glass disks that float in mid air. Several inverted conical shaped columns—clad in stainless steel—add to the futuristic look of the space as do the square columns covered with mirrored squares that not only reflect the razzle-dazzle of the lights and the metals but also gives a fractured replay of the wood inlay mural that spreads across one wall of the dining room. Six different kinds of natural wood veneers are set into the wall to recreate the interplay of geometric shapes.

The open food presentation stations are clad in stainless steel and they are highlighted by multi-colored mosaics. Here, the terrazzo floor sweeps out in a bold, splashy pattern of blue, red, orange and charcoal gray with the narrow end facing the serve stations and then fanning out towards the tables and chairs set behind the fanciful, sculpted railing.

INTERIOR DESIGN • ll X lV Design Associates, Toronto, ON
ARCHITECT • The Webb Zerafa Menkes Housden Partnership
PHOTOGRAPHY • David Whittaker

Bud Light Terrace

The Bud Light Terrace is part of the trinity of food options designed by Chute Gerdeman of Columbus for the Nationwide Arena in Columbus. The Arena is the home to the Columbus Bluejackets. The client, Sportservice's Facilities Management wanted something "different"—not what one typically finds in sports arenas. Denny Gerdeman, of the design firm, says, "Restaurants are retail—they have to create drama and entice customers. We wanted to work together to create a memorable experience for Nationwide Arena's visitors. Since they both agreed to what the goal was, what resulted was the Pizzuti Lounge & Club Bar shown earlier in this book and the food court which is shown here.

The 23,680 sq. ft. Bud Light Terrace food court is located on the main concourse and it was designed to relate to the Arena's architecture and the historic district the Arena is located in. The designers found their inspiration in the Pike Place

Market in Seattle, Fanieul Hall in Boston and Columbus' own North Market which is a major attraction for food epicures. The result is an open, eclectic collection of materials and graphics with a 1950s industrial feeling. A palette of retro colors and typestyles are used in combination with brushed aluminum and perforated metals. The school bus yellow, bright red orange and cool slate blue get an extra boost from the neon signage that sizzles over the assorted concession stands. Though the same basic materials and complementary colors are used, each station ends up with a distinctive look. It is these "graphic personalities" and the three dimensional qualities that allow visitors to quickly get themselves oriented and find what they are looking for. Each concession is "a landmark." Also, the shapes of the stands allows food service to be offered from several points at the same time thus "easing the pinch points often created by queue lines." "Westside Grill" is red hot while the Ice Cream stand glistens with cool blues and a back wall of shiny corrugated aluminum. The "Eastside Grill" gives off a more orange/gold glow while "Terrace Pizza" is readily recognized by the yellow towers to either side of the perforated metal and yellow tiled stand.

DESIGN • Chute Gerdemasn, Columbus, OH
PRINCIPAL • Denny Gerdeman
PROGRAM MANAGEMENT • Wendy Johnson
DESIGN • Andrew Hubbard
GRAPHIC DESIGN • Eric Daniel
GRAPHIC PRODUCTION • Susan Siewny
VISUAL MERCHANDISING • Heidi Brandewien & Nicole Vachow
DESIGN DOCUMENTATION • Steve Andreano
PROJECT COORDINATION • Ric Wolff
CLIENT TEAM
   GENERAL MANAGER • Jerry Freed
   VP BUILDING SERVICES • Jack Hertenstein
   SPORTSERVICE • Pia Nielsen
   PHOTOGRAPHY • StudiOhio, Columbus, OH

Freddies

Freddies is a classic example of where corporate cafeteria dining is headed. The evolution from the standard, dry, dull corporate lunch room with vending machines and limited options, to Freddies as shown here, indicates how far people's eating options have come in only a few short years. Dining, today, in many corporate cafés/cafeterias/dining rooms is often a culinary experience.

This corporate cafeteria in the Bayer Corporation's U.S. Headquarters building in Pittsburgh, PA is a "destination." "By giving the place a name, we began a process of branding that would create an identity consistent with the new kinds of services we planned to offer," said Allan Greenberg of Hospitality Services of Baltimore—the designers of Freddies. They selected the name Freddies for Friedrich Bayer who 130 years ago, with his partner Friedrich Weskott, formed the company that today employs over 14,000 people. With the Americanized name and designed with an eye to the increasingly sophisticated con-

sumers and driven by the need for fast, economic service, the restaurant style food service facility has quickly become the place to go for lunch and snacks. Diners can see their meals being prepared in the open prep areas and thus the dining experience becomes more interactive.

The space is divided into a series of stations or platforms and each is clearly identified so that the diner can quickly get

DESIGN • Hospitality Services,Inc., Baltimore, MD

ALLAN GREENBERG • Founder & President

INTERIOR DESIGNERS • Rockland Studios, Baltimore MD
   Wendy Goldman

ARCHITECTS • WTW Architects, Pittsburgh, PA
   Richard De Young, Sr. Principal

FOOD SERVICE MANAGEMENT • Parkhurst Dining Services,
   Pittsburgh, PA

NICK CARMODY • VP of Operations

PHOTOGRAPHY • Massery Photographers, Pittsburgh, PA
   Edward R. Massery

to where he/she wants to be. A brick pizza oven serves as the anchor for the Pizza/Pasta station where the diner can have a pizza "made to order." Hot entrees are available at the Bravisimo!/Sequoia Grill while the Street Deli serves up a range of sandwich and wrap options. Barista's is a full service coffee bar that offers pastries along with drinks and snacks to go. The Soup & Salad platform has other food selections for the diner-in-a-hurry. Using the platform style of design entices the diners to browse amid the many offerings. As Allan Greenberg puts it, "The idea is to come in and wander around checking out things and seeing what you'd like to eat." The

sights, sounds and smells of the foods being prepared also lead the diner through the space and the expert lighting picks out the very best of the offerings.

The seating possibilities are varied and offer friendly arrangements. Natural light comes in through the new sky-lights to brighten up the dining areas which include stand-up tables with tall stools, and banquet chairs and tables which are movable and can be reconfigured to suit the party's needs. Throughout, live plants serve as dividers as well as ornamenta-tion and enhance the out-of-doors dining concept. The net result is a more comfortable and inviting dining atmosphere.

T. Rowe Price Cafeteria

According to the design firm, Hospitality Services of Baltimore, Inc., "With work these days being 'virtually' everywhere, 'working' no longer implies the typical day at the office—and neither does eating." At the corporate dining room on the T. Rowe Price business campus, the designers created a bright, colorful dining retreat and food service which not only is time efficient but also offers a menu with lighter, more healthful choices as well as vegetarian options.

The free sweeping open service area includes a grill, deli, entree station, pizza/pasta station, a salad bar and a baker. The floor is laid with a very light gray ceramic tile and the curved servery counter is matte black with a stainless steel undulating tray track. The rear walls are also tiled but in bold areas of red,

orange, yellow and light gray. The pizza oven is on view and set into a curved sweep of red ceramic tiles. Accent walls, surrounding the service area, are highlighted in red and orange to complement the white walls and ceilings. The dining area is set apart behind a translucent wall of frosted glass. The large space is divided by the color patterns on the floor: part red and part pale gray and the spaces are delineated by the focal walls painted orange and blue.

The new cafeteria is capable of comfortably providing meals and refreshments for over 500 workers a day.

DESIGN • Hospitality Services, Inc., Baltimore, MD
PHOTOGRAPHY • Michael Dersin Photography.
Courtesy of HIS

Marconi Restaurant Court

Located in building #3 of a three-building complex of 300,000 sq. ft. is the Marconi Restaurant Court designed by Studios Architecture and Hospitality Services, Inc. The 355-seat, 18,000 sq,. ft. food service facility was created to appeal to the varied tastes, influences and schedules of a large employee group—and the food service area had to compete with the nearby local food retailers.

A high tech and individualistic feeling predominates throughout. The building's curving walls, open ducts and exposed light fixtures convey "a high energy, Silicon Valley" atmosphere. To underline the high tech feeling, corrugated steel and glazed curtain walls were used and to enhance the highly "individualistic" quality—there are no designated entrances and exits; traffic is free flowing. There are no lines and diners can approach from any direction.

A "kitchen forward" design brings the kitchen into the servery and customers can create their own meals at any of the five stations. Not only are the fresh foods displayed but one can watch the food being prepared. Typically, customers choose a selection from a great number of predetermined specials, go assemble other parts of their meal, and return to pick up their order. There is a free-flowing movement between the stations. There are no menu boards but "specials" are visible everywhere and custom, made-to-order meals can be requested.

The main stations include Pizza/Pasta where a wood fired brick oven is the focal point. On the counter top are a variety of cooked and baked offerings and home made pasta can be sauteed with the diner's choice of sauces, vegetables and seafood. An authentic working bakery dominates the Bakery/Deli area where breads, rolls and buns are freshly baked. Sandwiches, panini, subs, wraps and pitas are all prepared here as well. The Grill/Entree/Specialty Cooking is a large island suite with ranges, wok ranges, steamers, griddles, grills, fryers and ovens. Customers choose from a long display case filled with fish, seafood, prepared meats, and other fresh products. In addition to

the daily grilled special there is a stir-fried, Pacific/Asian specialty.

There is also a salad bar, a Grab-and-Go stop for ready made salads, sandwiches and snacks and a Coffee Shop. The Coffee Shop is the ideal place for a quick coffee break or snack when the cafeteria is closed.

Via Internet, Fore System's employees can read about the daily specials, and wall mounted video monitors in the offices enable the employees to check out the traffic flow in the cafeteria at any given time and thus plan their meal breaks.

DESIGN & PLANNING • Hospitality Services, Inc., Baltimore, MD

PRESIDENT • Allan Greenberg

PROJECT PRINCIPAL • Erik Sueberkrop, FAIA

ASSOC. PRINCIPAL/PROJECT ARCHITECT • Jerry Griffin, AIA

ASSOCIATE ARCHITECT • Alan W. Weiskopf, AIA, Perfido Weiskopf Arch., Pittsburgh, PA

PHOTOGRAPHY • Michael Dersin Photography. Courtesy of HIS

Harkness Commons

B ergmeyer Associates of Boston transformed what was a dark, depressing and outmoded cafeteria into the spacious, state-of-the-art dining environment shown here. Where previously students and faculty were limited to a single traffic path with few food choices, now they have many options beautifully presented in the expanded space. The servery is now open for exploration and there are temptations set out all along the way.

In consideration of the fact that the building that houses the cafeteria was originally designed by Walter Gropius, the noted architect, the designers at Bergmeyer renovated the space with respect and with inspiration garnered from the Bauhaus aesthetics of simplicity, regularity and geometry. The space is now fitted with fine, rich materials like the cherry wood facings on the granite topped serving counters and the distinctive wall of movable frosted glass panels which separates the servery from the adjacent seating area.

There is little contrast or "pizzazz" built into this elegant, refined servery. The walls behind the counters are paved with 8x8 in. gray tiles while small, light and medium gray glazed tiles clad the piers that delineate the various stations in the servery. Gray and black is used for the identifying signage over the stations and the menu boards follow the same Bauhaus inspired aesthetics in gray, white and black.

In the center of the servery is an oval salad bar finished with a steel and glass sneeze guard. The renovation has met with tremendous acceptance and the success has made the cafeteria a popular place to meet and eat.

DESIGN • Bergmeyer Associates, Boston, MA
PROJECT ARCHITECT • Nina Monastero, AIA
Jeanne Carey, AIA
PHOTOGRAPHY • Lucy Chen, Somerville, MA

Primo's/The New College Market

As part of Loyola College's desire to enhance its academic reputation and gain recognition as an outstanding classic Jesuit University, the College adopted a new perspective on its food facilities. Loyola College commissioned Hospitality Services, Inc. to head the effort and devise a college food experience that is unique to higher education and that would be compatible with the sophisticated tastes of college apartment dwellers. It would also have to compete with local restaurants.

Overwhelmingly the students especially expressed a desire for greater variety in food offerings, quality preparation, fresher and healthier foods, convenience and continuous service. The result is Primo's—The New College Market It was designed with the authenticity and the feel of a Euro-style market as opposed to a dining hall. It is an environment where students and faculty have options and formats to select from. The space

is divided into platforms. The platforms are sectioned by flexible food service concepts that offer a wide variety of solutions. The "Chef's Table" features a hot and grilled food menu. There are also the following food stations; Pizza/Pasta. The Delicatessen, The Barista, and The Garden Grocer. Each is relatively self sufficient from the storage, preparation and service aspects. Primo's Italian menu emanates from the Pizza/Pasta station and throughout the day fresh pastas, noodles, and sauces are prepared in the open kitchen to be sold in packages-to-go or to be sauteed or baked in casseroles. A large selection of related grocery items complement this station or platform.

According to the designers, "The facility has a very strong visual appeal. It was intended to be comfortable and relaxing for shopping or dining." The "timeless look" was created by the expansive use of natural woods and stone and a flexible and effective lighting plan was used to enhance the warmth of the space and also show off the food to its best advantage. "The architecture is meant to provide a believable and authentic background." Earth tones—rusts, browns and beiges—with accents of black, pewter, stainless steel and brick fill the servery and the various dining areas with the desired "warmth." Mosaic tiles in blue, orange, terra cotta and black outline the paths created by the faience baked tiles in front of

the assorted platforms. The all-important Chef's Table is distinguished by the rich blue glazed bricks on the rear wall of the prep area. Antiqued steel panels and mesh are combined with the elegant satin wood veneers for a most unique look.

There are four separate dining areas. The Terrace dining room, which seats about 150, is warm and intimate in feeling and it is a popular "hang out." The room is casual and comfortable with carpeted floors, shaded windows and upholstered seating to enhance "the clubby" look. A "low commitment" café area, near The Barista counter, can accommodate 40 for a quick cup of coffee—or a little more prolonged stay with a newspaper. The most spacious is the upstairs dining room which has 20 ft. windows and can seat 250. This area is especially useful for parties and/or larger groups and is available 24 hours a day.

Sales at Primo's have averaged $23,000 a day for this 3600 undergraduate student campus. That is 3600 transactions Monday through Friday and 2500 transactions a day on weekends. It has proven itself to be an unqualified success.

DESIGN & PLANNING • Hospitality Services, Inc., Baltimore, MD

PRESIDENT • Allan Greenberg

INTERIOR DESIGNER • Wendy Goldman

ARCHITECT • Cochran, Stephenson & Donkervoet, Inc.

PRINCIPAL IN CHARGE • Thomas Spies

PROJECT MANAGER • John C. Morrell, AIA

OWNER'S REP • O'Brien Kreitzberg at Loyola College, John Hill

PHOTOGRAPHY • Maxwell MacKenzie Architectural Photography, Washington, DC, Courtesy of HIS

Boulder Garden Café

Though Loyola College has recently opened the very successful Primo's another food facility was needed and again Hospitality Services, Inc. came to the design rescue. This space is located at the center of an emerging campus retail-plex with neighbors such as TicketMaster, a book store, a fully equipped cyber center and a conference center. "We needed to create branded concepts that would cut through the clutter," said Allan Greenberg, president of HIS. "We wanted Boulder Garden Café to be sufficiently distinctive not to be perceived as a 'mini-Primo's'." The designers also did not want to create a traditional retail food court.

The result is four "home" brands created by HIS because, as Greenberg says, "most of us have come to actually prefer some kind of 'brand identity' to go with our dining choices, if only to tell us what to anticipate from the menu." The grill station is now "Phil's Grill" and it is also a sort of diner with black and white vertically striped walls and dubonnet trim. It features a Baltimore-flavored menu with crab cakes, boardwalk style fries, gourmet burgers and assorted grilled sandwiches. "Phil's Grill" has a definite look and the design goes from the layout and finish of the space to the menu, the signage and

even the server outfits—"to create a convincing 'brand feel' in the mind of the customers."

"Star Deli" focuses on deli subs, distinctive soups and imaginative condiments. The deli meats, cheeses and salads are showcased in refrigerated cases and the oven is prominent in the design.

"Pizza Pies" stands out with its Mediterranean blue tiled surfaces, custom lighting and the logo—a series of vertical ovals rendered in a fashionable modern palette. "You imagine it and we'll make it" makes pizza selections a challenge—there are so many options.

"Surf'n'Joe" was designed especially for the hurried student or faculty member. Under a coffee cup with legs riding a surfboard is a selection of sandwiches, fresh fruit drinks, milk shakes and coffee. The bright orange, teal and green colors can not go unnoticed. "Taco Bell," a national brand, was added as a brand that complements Boulder Garden Café's signature brands.

"The overall look is a very coffee-right feel for a college campus. It's fun, whimsical and decidedly easygoing"—and it is a work-in-progress with menu selections evolving based on consumer reactions.

DESIGN & PLANNING • Hospitality Services, Inc., Baltimore, MD

PRESIDENT • Allan Greenberg

PHOTOGRAPHY • Courtesy of HIS

CALZONES

Cheese Filled.............. $
Each Topping.............. $
Breadsticks............... $
with marinara sauce
Add Mozzarella Cheese.. $

PIZZA PIES

Individual 8" Pizza Pie.... $
Each Topping.............. $

sausage, ham, pepperoni, olives,
green peppers, mushrooms, garlic,
onions, tomato, extra cheese

PIZZA
PIES

NAIT Cafeteria

NORTH ALBERTA INSTITUTE OF TECHNOLOGY, EDMONTON, AB

Working with Marrack + Associates Inc., Jon Sunderland of Sunderland Innerspace Design developed a unique concept for the main dining room area of North Alberta Institute of Technology (NAIT) in Edmonton, AB in Canada. Together they formulated a "market approach which offers the selection of food in a modular and informal setting." "This market approach enhances the quality of the product, the variety of selection, and encourages creative merchandising of food." Jon Sunderland also says, "The servery is a collection of various sized food stations that act independently. Skewing the orientation of the food stations promotes individuality while providing an opportunity to merchandise product and promote the idea of freshness and variety to the customer."

Marmoleum, laid in a free form checkerboard, is reminiscent of a deli or kitchen floor and it also sets the tone for the friendly environment. The deep, earthy red and yellow-beige appears in a harlequin pattern behind the service counters and they are combined with the rich blue of the ceiling, on the freestanding columns and on the floor. Combined with the tiles, the marmoleum and the assorted laminate facings are the quilted panels of shiny metal that recall the diners of the 1950s. Here the material is used on the fascia over the serveries. Stained fiberboard wood finishes are used for most of the fixtures and the servery components to further the "market" flavor.

A suspended medite paneled ring floats over the center of the space and together with stretched Teflon sail cloth on wall and ceiling areas plus the use of railing define the seating area. The designers were "able to visually interrupt the vast space to create intimacy and a sense of comfort." Large food inspired murals are used to highlight the space and they are executed in the same, warm, contrasting color palette.

The designers of this project were recognized by the Foodservice Consultants Society International (FCSI) with the "Award for Excellence in Design."

DESIGN • Sunderland Innerspace Design, Vancouver, BC
(now Smart Design)
Jon Sunderland, Principal/Designer and Marrack + Associates, Inc.
PHOTOGRAPHY • Ross Germanluk Photography,
Edmonton, AB

Rand Hall

With students and faculty seeking off-campus dining because the Rand Hall dining facility was so old, uninspired and downright boring, Vanderbilt University decided to do something about the situation. The design firm of Gresham Smith and Partners was called upon to create a magic turnabout—and a new image.

Under the supervision of James Harding, Director of Environmental Graphics at the design firm, the project took off. Though the project included architectural, interior and electrical disciplines "our graphic group took the lead in the overall design concept." Time was of the essence too. The renovation had to be completed by the time the students returned from their summer break. This gave Gresham Smith only three weeks to come up with a concept and seven more weeks to realize it. In addition to

the time constraint there was a limited budget available for the makeover. The general theme that evolved was based on a market place concept. "For a fraction of retail cost our team of designers purchased old doors, windows, wrought iron, cast iron vents and various and sundry items from reuse centers and second hand stores to create the desired character and atmosphere."

The result is a fun and frolicing "stage set"; a food court where the eight individual concessions have bright and attractive personalities that somehow blend to create an exciting ambiance just right for the collegiate diners. Drinks are available at a pump station which is distinguished by the giddy artwork of old-fashioned gas pumps which now dispense milk, H20, Soda, etc. The pre-prepared meals-to-go are located in an old VW bus that has been cut in half, refrigeration added along with stickers that play up the amusing brand name of "Vango." The background is a

custom mural that uses Van Gogh's Café Terrace as its inspiration. All the concession menu boards and signs are colorful and whimsical and add to the overall fun marketplace atmosphere.

Sales are up by 50% and the new concept is definitely working.

DESIGN • Gresham, Smith & Partners, Nashville, TN

PRINCIPAL IN CHARGE • Jim Harding

PROJECT MANAGER • Craig Berry

ARCHITECT • Jason East

FOR VANDERBILT UNIVERSITY

   FRANK GLADU • Dir. Of Dining Services

   PHOTOGRAPHY • Brian Robbins, Suwanee, GA

Varsity Beach

The Branscomb Quadrangle is the Freshmen's residence hall at Vanderbilt University and Varsity Beach/Munchi Mart is located here. The 3000 sq. ft. area combines a convenience store, a mini food court and a coffee house all in one. The area is especially popular as a dinner and late night dining option. Over 2000 people visit Varsity Beach on an average school day.

The designers at Gresham, Smith and Partners were commissioned to create a "hang out" that would be a safe place for the students to be but also be the kind of place they would want to hang out.

Offered in the colorful surroundings are Vanderbilt's own food brands; Muffin Tin Bakery, Decco's Diner, Rocket Subs and Vango Grab-and-go sandwiches and salads. Also located in Varsity Beach are Papa John's Pizzas and a Ben & Jerry Ice

Cream outlet. The space is cool and clean; predominantly white, gray and black accented with the school's signature blue color. The gray and white checkerboard patterned floor is highlighted with black squares and black chairs are pulled up to the round, whiter laminate topped tables. A giant mural stretches across one wall and it is filled with students doing student things. Directly under the mural is a long counter with diner-style stools upholstered in the fresh colors of the mural which is another seating option. Another student activity mural adds "people" and a sense of fun to the separate dining area which is painted a grayed-down aqua. The same color is used here as the floor accent. The sliced up and refrigerated VW van appears at Varsity Beach to transport cool selections to-go.

In addition, non food items purchased in the C-store in Varsity Beach make up 25% to 30% of the total merchandise sold here.

DESIGN • Gresham, Smith & Partners, Nashville, TN

PRINCIPAL IN CHARGE/DIR. OF

ENVIRONMENTAL GRAPHICS • James Harding

PHOTOGRAPHY • Brian Robbins Photography, Suwanee, GA

The Visual Reference Library

of Architecture and Design

Visit

www.visualreference.com

Index by design firm